Mason Gaffney

Mason Gaffney is a national treasure. He boldly treads where few other economists even dare to peek: at the extraction of rent from the many by the few. Such rent extraction is now massive and threatens to destroy our democracy. To those who wonder how to stop it, my advice is simple: read Gaffney.

— *Peter Barnes, author of* Capitalism 3.0 *and* The Sky Trust

Mason Gaffney has taught generations of urban planners and economists to appreciate how taxing land can improve cities, the economy, and the environment. His rare combination of theoretical rigor, political passion, and clear writing impressed me early in my own academic career. This wonderful collection of his incisive essays will educate and entertain everyone who wants to know more about land and taxes.

— *Donald Shoup, Distinguished Professor of Urban Planning, UCLA*

While too much his own man to be a disciple, Mason Gaffney is widely known as the leading active Georgist economist. This selection of his extensive writings provides an excellent introduction to his body of thought. All apply economics to the design of a more productive economy and a fairer society, and most discuss how expanding land taxation can go far in achieving these goals. These stimulating and thought-provoking articles are written with flair, elegance, and erudition.

— *Richard Arnott, University of California, Riverside*

In 1970, I was an uppity Nader's Raider, on the trail of giant California land barons. I stumbled on a hilarious account of California's preposterous irrigation system with its crisscrossing canals. I just had to meet the author, so I tracked Mason down in Washington, DC, where he then worked for Resources for the Future. He invited me and my ex to dinner, fried us up hamburgers with soy sauce, sang Gilbert and Sullivan tunes with his own words, and sent us on our way with reprints and the dictum, "Tax capital and labor and you drive them away; tax land and you drive it into use!" That meeting led me to study economics in Mason's old department at UC Berkeley, and into a lifetime of learning from him.

— *Mary M. Cleveland, Columbia University*

If the Nobel Prize Committee ever returns to its original mission of awarding prizes for research that benefits society, they should give serious consideration to the life's work of Mason Gaffney. He has shown how to create a peaceful, prosperous economy that does not depend on imperialism or exploitation.

— *Clifford Cobb, author, historian*

Gaffney is the preeminent scholar of what's ailing our economy and how to revitalize it with job opportunities and decent living standards for all Americans.

— *Walt Rybeck, Director, Center for Public Dialogue; author of* Re-Solving the Economic Puzzle

Mason Gaffney is the greatest economist the world has never heard of. Professor Gaffney supplies a theory of public finance that shows why Western economies overexploit natural resources, underemploy labor, lurch from crisis to crisis and are prone to ever-widening disparities of wealth. He explains why neither "liberal" demand-side stimulus nor "conservative" supply-side fiscal policies have suceeded. Mason Gaffney's analysis has never been refuted; it has simply been ignored. Somehow, remarkably, he has maintained his cheery optimism and side-splitting humor, so evident in these essays.

— *Kris Feder, Bard College*

Mason Gaffney is the rare economist who looks for practical solutions. Gaffney explains how taxing land rather than buildings can generate local government revenue and promote urban infill development, greater employment, and overall urban revitalization

— results urban planners have long advocated. Gaffney also lays out ways to counteract leapfrogging sprawl, the nation's leading land use problem, through removing public subsidies. He shows why cities should also adopt land value taxation as an incentive to create more compact and economically robust communities.

— *Thomas Daniels, University of Pennsylvania*

Mason Gaffney's insightful writings on public finance, the structure of capital goods, and the business cycle are a bolt of enlightenment, in contrast to the dreary and almost useless mainstream thought that treats symptoms rather than causes. You cannot find better economic writing than that of Professor Mason Gaffney.

— *Fred Foldvary, San Jose State University*

Prof. Gaffney writes about important questions, with elegance, clarity and wit. I always enjoy reading his papers. When I refer to one of them to check on a point, I often find myself re-reading the whole paper, because I find it so engaging. When I read other economists I find errors in their thinking. That doesn't seem to happen when I read Mason Gaffney's work.

— *Nicolaus Tideman, Virginia Polytechnic Institute*

Here is an economist that the vast majority of our tribe is too defectively educated to understand. Economics is not the dismal science; it is we economists who are dismal, because we have lost our imagination. One need not agree with everything that Mason says to marvel at the depth of his mind and the reach of his wit. We have here marvelous observations and comments upon the timeless necessity of "getting and spending."

— *Daniel Bromley, Professor Emeritus, University of Wisconsin-Madison; Editor,* Land Economics

Most economists neither really understand their subject nor love its history. Mason Gaffney's love of truth and the history of economics pervades what he has written. One of my few regrets in life is not having been closer than 7,650 miles away from Mason Gaffney to discuss in detail crucial derailments in economic thought and tax policy, such as John Bates Clark's (absurdly successful) fraudulent attempt to pretend that land is merely man-made capital.

— Dr. Terry Dwyer, Economist, lawyer, Former Tax advisor to the Australian Prime Minister

If you have ever wondered why big cities have empty lots while development sprawls far into what was once farmland, Mason Gaffney's essays will explain it all in clear and upbeat terms. For decades Gaffney has led the Georgist movement that seeks to tax land, but not buildings, to foster the best use of land while ending the subtle, and corrosive, redistribution of wealth to owners of real estate. Even if you disagree with Mase his insights will bring new clarity to economics.

— David Cay Johnston, Pulitzer Prize winning tax journalist

Mason Gaffney is an ideal "liberal arts" economist: Question everything, especially your own views; use common sense; be open about your judgments, and encourage debate by stating your conclusions boldly. I don't always agree with him, but I always learn from him.

— David Colander, Middlebury College

Gaffney's instructive case histories brilliantly probe beneath the surface of economic phenomena to expose what modern economic analysis has lost by downplaying land values as the primary source of unearned riches. He reveals how current fiscal regimes increasingly privilege unearned income and wealth while penalizing production and harming the poor with regressive sales taxes.

— Roger Sandilands, Emeritus Professor of Economics, University of Strathclyde, Glasgow, Scotland

The scope, scale and quality of Prof. Mason Gaffney's anthology are truly breathtaking. This little gem will be on my students' required reading list with a note: "They don't make economists this way anymore." Yes, unfortunately, when they made Mase, they broke the mold.   *— Steve H. Hanke, The Johns Hopkins University*

The
Mason
Gaffney
Reader

Essays on Solving
the "Unsolvable"

HENRY GEORGE INSTITUTE

To my dear wife Ruth Letitia ("Tish"):
ever loyal, supportive,loving, energetic,
compatible, and tolerant of my ambitions
along with my need to nap now and then.
In fact, she is (and there is no higher
praise in economics) optimal!

The author and editor wish to thank Polly Cleveland and Wyn Achenbaum for their diligent and insightful help in creating this book.

The author thanks Nadine Stoner for selflessly offering him a forum for many of these essays, and never getting possessive about them.

The Mason Gaffney Reader:
    Essays on Solving the "Unsolvable"

by Mason Gaffney

edited, with an introduction, by Lindy Davies

isbn   978-0-9741844-6-3

Library of Congress Control Number   2013944493

Contents

Mason Gaffney:
The Great Elucidator

Mason Gaffney likes lists; he catalogues with gusto. At their best, his lists rival the sweep and grandeur of that master cataloguer, Walt Whitman. Gaffney's lists, like Whitman's, always serve to make a good thing better, reeling off one cogent surprise after another, and then some more!

The catalogue is an effective device for Mason Gaffney, particularly for the sort of writing collected here: essays for general readers, eschewing math and in-house discussions. Catalogues work for Gaffney because, in the main, he writes to elucidate a point that has long been obscured, by social scientists of every stripe, and yet is momentously important to society: the economic role of natural resources and opportunities — of land. It is an insight that ramifies profusely. Indeed, the opportunity to expose something so undeniable — and yet so prominently and repeatedly denied — affords delicious rhetorical possibilities, as in the following paragragh in which Prof. Gaffney compares real estate values in rich vs. poor neighborhoods in British Columbia:

> *Now do us both a favor, please. Pause and savor that comparison. Let it linger, as though you were testing a slow sip of wine from Fredonia's famous grapes. Roll it on your tongue, mull sensually over its aroma and bouquet, and, getting back to business, mull cerebrally over its full import. The house that shelters the very*

rich family is worth 2.8 times the house of the modest family; but the land under the house of the very rich is worth 17.5 times the land of the modest. Seventeen and one half times as much! Again, it is lot value, more than building value, that divides the rich from the poor. Seldom will you find an economic rule more strongly supported by data. It's just a matter of presenting the data so as to test and bring out the rule.[*]

Gaffney writes about other stuff too, of course. His published works include three books and hundreds of articles in peer-reviewed journals, essays, lectures and class notes. He has researched and written on the economics of forests, the environment, water, urban development, economic history and international relations. Yet the land — how it is owned, controlled, collateralized, its rents captured — has been the red thread that runs through every patch.

Mason Gaffney recently retired from active teaching at the University of California, Riverside, at age 90 — with his wits fully intact: three of the essays in this collection were written this year. Prior to Riverside, he was a Professor of Economics at several Universities, a journalist with TIME, Inc., a researcher with Resources for the Future, Inc., the head of the British Columbia Institute for Economic Policy Analysis, which he founded, and an economic consultant to several businesses and government agencies.

Given the radical insights that Gaffney has propounded throughout his career, it's amazing that he rose as high in the profession as he did. Over the years he found that the subjects that most interested him were precisely the ones best left unexplored by young economists seeking advancement. In a recent essay[†] he recalled being invited to join an Air Conservation Commission in the late 1950s.

Hardly any economists at that time had any interest in air pollution; they dismissed it and like matters as "externalities,"

---

[*] "The Taxable Capacity of Land," available at http://masongaffney.org/publications/G29-TaxableCapacityofLand.pdf
[†] "Sleeping with the Enemy: Economists Who Side with Polluters" in the first two issues of *Groundswell*, 2011, Common Ground-USA

outside their narrow realm of markets for "commodities." So, for lack of anyone more senior... this writer [was picked].... [At our] first meeting... each of us was asked to suggest a postulate on which we could all agree, as a foundation for further dialogue. I suggested that "Air is common property." Shocked silence! They didn't know whose property it is, but weren't ready for anything so, well, common, and who was I, anyway?

By the 1990s, mainstream economics was coming in for some pretty harsh criticism. It was labeled "autistic" — obsessed with self-consistency and increasingly abstruse mathematics. The field had come no closer to resolving the long-unanswered questions of political economy, and its most eminent practitioners seemed fine with that. Theorists such as Coase, Laffer, Stigler and Friedman won renown for theories that, made into policies, consolidated the gains of the rich. No distinction was to be tolerated between the earned incomes of labor and capital goods, and the unearned gains of privilege. "Capital" could be physical, or human, or financial — and land, outside that totally fungible realm, didn't exist at all. The more Gaffney looked into the provenance of these ideas, the more the field's descent into self-referential irrelevance seemed intentional. If, he reasoned, there existed a large and growing political movement bent on exposing and ending landed privilege (and there did) — and if the prestigious universities of that time, funded by oil and railroad barons, wished to devise an academic system to blunt and diffuse the influence of those progressive forces (and they did) — why, what they came up with would look a whole lot like neoclassical economics. Mason Gaffney's seminal work "Neoclassical Economics as a Stratagem Against Henry George," published in 1994 as *The Corruption of Economics,* told a story that needed telling — albeit one that no other insider seemed willing to stick his neck out and tell.

My own 20-some years in the Georgist movement has come toward the end of Mason's long career. I encountered him as an avuncular, unhurried, preoccupied sage. He can hit big-league pitching, yet he has never been impatient with boneheaded questioners (such as myself); if folks exhibit more zeal for justice, perhaps, than practical competence, he'll still work with them. He has generously shared his work, time and insights with those who wish to advance the principles that Henry George set forth in *Progress and Poverty*. He has no time for cynicism and hypocrisy, but has long been patient with bumptiousness.

Most of the essays in this book appeared in a forum that some, indeed, would call "bumptious" — The *Georgist Journal*. This magazine goes out to members of the world's three largest Georgist organizations. Such groups are devoted, in multifarious ways and styles, to spreading "the Georgist philosophy" and implementing the collection of land rent for public revenue, and the removal of taxes that burden production. They include many "true believers" whose high-volume zeal might be seen as an albatross 'round the neck of a serious economist and writer. Nevertheless, Mason Gaffney has steadfastly supported this rag-tag movement over the years. He doesn't accept error without complaint, but his (mostly) judicious corrections are offered without condescension. It's a sort of unassailable, humble authority that comes from really, really knowing what one is talking about.

This Georgist movement finds itself, in the 21st century, wobbling back to its feet after numerous setbacks. One of its vulnerabilities — which is, yet, also a source of strength — is its long tradition of autodidacticism and disdain for intellectual authority. This spirit traces back to Henry George himself, a high-school dropout and jack-of-all-trades who rose to become a major political voice and influential economic theorist. George's style has a messianic flavor — he was not about to mince words about the land question! The fervor rubbed off on many of George's followers. In later years they became caricatured as zealots who think there's only one important book about economics. Mason Gaffney's willingness to engage with all who care about the land question has been invaluable to the Georgist movement, both in terms of morale and of intellectual substance.

Though Gaffney is obviously deeply influenced by George, he is not shy about pointing out — and constructively building on — the errors he finds in George's works. In this he has performed an indispensable service. Many have commented on Henry George's deficiencies in capital theory, and on the precise mechanism of boom/bust cycles. Almost all, however, have mentioned these things in passing. This creates two problems. Some seize on these fairly obvious mistakes, using them to dismiss all of George's work as naïve. Others ignore them, teaching a chapter-and-verse reading of George's books that gets them dismissed as cultists. Mason Gaffney's essays clear away the fog of such fantasies and get to the real issues. Thus, his work serves to correct the simplistic errors of both camps and to highlight the vital relevance of an updated form of Georgism — now called "Geoism" by many — to the most serious economic, social and environmental questions of our day.

All of these themes come together in Gaffney's recent essays, in which he considers economic themes over long historical time-frames, identifying the universal themes within superficially different contexts. For example, the essay "Europe's Fatal Affair with the Value-Added Tax" is far more than an explanation of the economics of sales taxes. It becomes a meditation on the age-old question of *what belongs* to individuals, and *what belongs* to communities. He shows how the views of the Physiocrats, the French *economistes* of the 18th century, had far-reaching influence on the US's founding fathers, and on the American economy to this day. Public, societal choices with regard to this question have consequences, and Gaffney's long historical view shows that these consequences are more predictable than many (particularly modern economists) would have you believe.

Likewise, in "Reverberations," he delves into history to illuminate, as few others have done, the inner workings of the "business cycle." In 1933, Ferdinand Pecora, an unknown prosecutor chosen at the last minute, had the audacity to ask rational questions, in hearings before the US Senate — which paved the way for the banking regulations that ushered in unprecedented growth and prosperity in the United States. Unfortunately, however, Pecora's investigations stopped short of uncovering real estate's crucial role in the boom/bust cycle. This essay is the best — bar none — brief exposition of the mechanics of macroeconomic cycles, and should be required reading for every econ major.

One last point before you get to the good stuff: Mason Gaffney's work as an economist is deeply important, but he gives you more: his work as a wordsmith, and as a whimsical, eclectic historian, is delightful. He might send you to your dictionary from time to time, as he did for me with his unusual use of "compose," in the sense of the *American Heritage Dictionary's* fifth definition, "to settle (arguments); reconcile"— in a way that even alludes to its fourth, "to make (one's mind or body) calm or tranquil" (c.f. the title of the final essay in this collection). Dear Reader, you're in for a treat: there's deep wisdom here, snazzily expressed.

— *Lindy Davies, June 2013*

Note on Documentation

Having spent his career as a professional economist and university professor, Mason Gaffney's habit is to thoroughly, even obsessively, document his work. The essays in this collection have been edited for general readers, and we have omitted their long lists of references. Those references are well worth reviewing, however. These essays — and much more — can be found in full-length, fully-documented versions at Prof. Gaffney's website, **www.masongaffney.org.**   — *L. D.*

Lindy Davies is the Program Director of the Henry George Institute, and author of The Alodia Scrapbook, *and of the online courses at* **www.henrygeorge.org.**

Taking the Professor for a Ride

From The Freeman, *November, 1942: "The writer of this article, Mason Gaffney, is a young Chicago Georgist who recently matriculated at Harvard. Perusal of the piece suggests that Freshman Gaffney's chances of becoming teacher's pet in the economics class are decidedly slim."*

Unruffled, composed, like a patient father straightening out a wayward son, he said, "You see, my boy, this Henry George lived at a time when the country was growing rapidly, when land values were skyrocketing and great fortunes were being made from speculation. Not being a 'trained economist,' George attached disproportionate importance to this... er... er... land question. Land is, of course, of minor importance in economics, and speculation, well... of trifling significance."

I should like to take this man, my "economics" teacher at Harvard, for a ride from the North Shore area near Chicago straight west on Illinois 58. A well built-up residential district, one-half to a mile deep, runs far north along the lake shore, to end abruptly in a wilderness of sidewalks, street signs, fire plugs and weeds — but no buildings. Along the roads which gridiron this wasteland speed trucks and pleasure cars, burning gas, tires and time to bridge the miles which, to no purpose, stand between the metropolis and outlying communities.

"Yes," my boss told me as we were riding to work one day, "there was a time when we thought there would be a lot of building out here. Guess I've still got some Land Company bonds in the Wilmette Bank. The company gave the farmer one-third down and agreed to pay the rest when the land was sold. Lots of poor farmers have got the land back now, with stiff taxes to pay on the improvements. Improvements, hell! Those fire plugs don't even have water pipes attached to them."

Ten miles of this and we reach Des Plaines, an oasis called by the natives a "successful development." "Thirty-one minutes to the Loop," boasts the Northwestern R. R. "These Homesites Best Speculation in Chicago Land," exults the land promoter.

Five miles farther west, about fifteen miles from Lake Michigan, the land is at last completely given over to farms. The speculator fires a parting shot at us as we reach the junction with Arlington Heights Road. "The Idle Rich of Today Bought Acres Yesterday," reads his sign.

Yes, I would like to ride with this "economist" out here. He would have trouble then convincing me that speculation is of trifling significance. Probably he would say: "But the men who hold this land are men of great foresight, very valuable men. You can't refuse to reward foresight; it's a virtue. Of course a little planning might alleviate these dreadful conditions but, tut, tut, my boy, do you want to destroy free enterprise?"

Reward foresight indeed! Foresight in itself deserves no economic reward. Hitler and Baby-face Nelson at times showed great foresight, yet their loot is by no means sanctified on that account. Only one kind of exertion deserves an economic reward, and that is exertion directed toward the gratification of human desires. Foresight, an attribute of labor, exerted in producing wealth, deserves a reward, and in the free market will bring a reward. But foresight no more justifies speculation in land than superior firepower justifies conquest.

Perhaps it is asking too much to expect a Harvard man to

understand this, however. His salary, after all, is paid in part from the proceeds of the foresight of certain friends of the institution who bought up much of the land on which the slums and business districts of Cambridge now stand.

⊰◆⊱

The author reflects: I had just turned 19, and received Greetings from Uncle Sam. Funny how fast one catches on, with the evidence lying outdoors all around you; and funny how southern California today replicates Chicagoland in 1942. Funny, too, how economics profs had their ways of signaling you that looking into land speculation was, well, just not done in elite circles. How little progress we have made since then in understanding and coping with this phenomenon and its derivative ills.

Eighteen Answers to Futilitarians

Constructive problem-solving is when one takes problems and dilemmas and composes them into solutions. A simple example is when two lonely, longing people meet and marry. Another, more prosaic, is when a producer converts wastes into useful by-products. Another, more general, is whenever demand meets supply.

The genius of Henry George was to confront dismal dilemmas, futile standoffs and harsh trade-offs posed by what we may call "futilitarians," and compose or reconcile them into solutions. The most obvious such desperate trade-off he solved was that posed by Malthus, who told the working classes they must choose between food and sex.

Today, futilitarian economists have an array of dismal choices for us: equity vs. efficiency; attracting business vs. supporting public services; inflation vs. unemployment; pollution vs. unemployment; equality vs. incentives; productivity vs. full employment; equality vs. saving and capital formation; free choice vs. urban sprawl; etc.

Understanding George's program, one can see that those allegedly hard choices are false, calculated to unman us and make resolute action seem futile. Herewith is a list of reconciliations that are inherent in George's philosophy.

George's ideas are more than a philosophy, they are a

prescription for action. For short, I shall describe his public policy program as "Geofiscalism." For George, a philosophy was designed to accompany a program of action: theory and practice were also composed and reconciled. He saw theory and practice (or thought and action) as complements, not substitutes. So should we.

1. Geofiscalism composes common rights in land with private tenure of land, and free markets. It tends, on balance, to foster subdivision of land. Those still excluded from tenure are compensated in three ways: landowners support government; they must hire workers and invest in new capital to generate income from their lands; and they must supply goods and services from the land. The last two combine the stimuli of supply-side and demand-side economics, leveling them upwards. The Keynesian specter of oversaving is dispelled by untaxing capital, stimulating new investments.

2. Geofiscalism untaxes labor without raising taxes on capital, or capital formation. It is even possible to untax both labor and capital, while still supporting government at high levels, or distributing the surplus as a social dividend.

3. Geofiscalism composes equity with efficiency. It is pro-incentive, for reasons well known. At the same time the tax base, land, is highly concentrated among the wealthiest people, including alien owners and nimble international tax-dodgers. Thus it combines the pro-incentive effects of a poll tax with the equalizing effects of a progressive wealth tax.

4. Local and regional (state, provincial) governments can pay for public services as generously as they please while simultaneously attracting industry, capital and population by untaxing them.

5. Geofiscalism contains urban sprawl without denying consumers free choice of location. It lets settlement be contained within growth boundaries, if desired, without inequity, by making the favored landowners pay most of the taxes; it lets settlers choose outlying locations, if they wish, by making them pay the incremental social costs they impose on the whole.

6. Geofiscalism creates jobs without use of inflationary demand stimulus. It stimulates both supply and demand jointly, leveling them upwards (cf. #1). It proffers us "True Fiscal Stimulus," in contrast to the current shallow usage of "fiscal stimulus" to mean deficit finance and bank expansion.

7. Geofiscalism lets a polity attract people without diluting its resource base. We may label this the "Hong Kong Effect," although it is observable in most thriving cities. It results from the power of economic synergy in free markets to generate large economic surpluses, surpluses that lodge in the rent and value of local land, such that large, densely settled cities generally have more land value *per capita* than smaller cities and farm regions. George summarized this force as resulting from "Association in Equality"; and he clearly meant *free* association, free of taxes on exchange, and with equal rights to land. A modern planner would want to elaborate on the efficient circulation systems and layouts to facilitate such association, and George would surely agree; but he would remind the modern planner, as he reminded his contemporary civil engineers, that taxes on exchange offset and penalize the very linkages that good planning and public works strive to achieve.

8. Geofiscalism makes jobs while abating demands on nature and the environment. This is a byproduct of containing urban sprawl (cf. #5, #9), and the Hong Kong Effect (#7). The synergistic city is resource-sparing.

More generally, Geofiscalism puts a new focus on raising the productivity of land and natural resources, in contrast with the current unbalanced, exclusive focus on maximizing labor productivity, even at the unspoken cost of wasting land.

Geofiscalism is also philosophically compatible with "green taxes," which are based on a philosophy that nature belongs to all in common, and those who poach on it and defile it should pay society for what they take, and the damage they do. George himself did not develop this theme, but latter-day Geofiscalists have done so, using the economist's tool of "marginal cost pricing," which shows the efficiency both of land-value taxes and of green taxes.

9. Geofiscalism promotes economy in government. By making jobs, it automatically lowers welfare costs, both directly by taking people off the dole, and indirectly by weakening the rationale for most doles in the first place. Making jobs of course lowers crime, with all its direct and indirect costs. It lowers social unrest, with threats of riots and arson.

It also abates the high costs, both civil and military, of territorial expansion. Now, such expansion results from three forces combined: people seeking jobs and lands; investors seeking outlets; and land speculators seeking unearned increments. Geofiscalism abates all three forces by directing human settlement and activity to a smaller area of better lands.

As a happy byproduct, this also abates demands on nature and the environment.

10. Geofiscalism lets us raise tax rates without impairing the tax base: there is no "Laffer-curve Effect." That is, higher tax rates must always yield higher tax levies.[*]

11. Geofiscalism effects a radical social and economic reform in a completely non-catastrophic way, working silently through existing institutions and the free market. It can be and has been adopted (in part) by democratic governments, by authoritarian ones (Meiji Japan), and by foreign occupying forces (MacArthur Japan, Kuomintang Taiwan, Hong Kong, Kiauchow).

12. Geofiscalism may be and has been applied by local, central, and intermediate levels of government.

---

[*] There is a "tax capitalization effect" such that a rise in the tax rate may yield a less than proportionate rise in the tax levy; but that should not be confused with a Laffer-curve Effect.

13. Geofiscalism may be and has been applied in whole or in part. It is compatible with a mixed economy. It may be applied immediately, or phased in slowly, as preferred.

14. Geofiscalism is impervious to tax-avoidance and evasion schemes: foreign tax havens, tax shelters, profit shifting, concealment, electronic transfers, smuggling, creative accounting, etc. Every parcel of land is open for inspection. It lies unambiguously within one taxing jurisdiction. It cannot be moved or hidden. The owners must identify themselves, pay up, or lose their land. Foreign residents and foreign owners have no advantage over resident citizens.

15. Geofiscal levies are enforceable without tracing persons, and without threatening them with jail or other personal penalties. The land is the hostage.

16. Geofiscalism democratizes access to land, in the manner of open access to a commons, yet without relaxing the constraint on economic use. It democratizes and opens up access by lowering the purchase price; it puts a constraint on wasteful holdings by imposing an annual charge or tax on holding land. The net effect is the same as making credit available to all potential buyers on exactly the same terms: same rate of interest for all, and perpetual credit for all. Land credit is extended to the poor, and everyone, with no risk of non-repayment.

It also puts future buyers on the same footing as the present owners, thus removing the differential advantage of inherited entitlements. This last point does not, of course, commend itself to most of those with inherited entitlements, yet in many circumstances even they will experience gains, if the advantage of lowering other taxes exceeds the rise in the land tax.

17. Geofiscalism speeds the renewal of sites now occupied or covered by decayed and/or obsolete machinery, equipment and buildings. It does so without subsidies, either direct ones to new equipment or indirect ones like sacrificing tax revenues. Thus it keeps a nation's physical plant modern and competitive, hastening the embodiment of new technology into working material forms. It increases investment opportunities at home, providing outlets and stores of value for savings.

18. Geofiscalism raises revenue without any complex machinery and paperwork such as bedevil the income taxes (corporate and personal), and without any confidentiality of tax data from the press and the public. No one but the tax man knows what special income tax deals are enjoyed by anyone else; it's all personal and confidential, and wide open to corruption. Land, on the other hand, is public business.

Panacea?

George, considering such reconciliations, wrote in wonder that "The laws of the universe are harmonious."* Modern philosophers may cavil at his mode of expression and his awe, but that need not distract us. Perhaps the harmony came from his attitude, his problem-solving orientation, as much as from the universe, but in either case it is real enough, and wonderful to realize. Let us adopt the same attitude, and watch our intractable problems fall away.

Some captious critics, viewing just a few of such claims of harmony, damn Geofiscalism as a "panacea." The word betrays a curiously warped mindset: who would damn a solution for the very reason that it is a solution? The word is theirs, though, and what they evidently mean is only implied: strong claims must be false, by assumption, so the critics are spared from proving them false in any specific way. That is counterfeit wisdom, indeed, and a cop-out. It is our fortuity as Geofiscalists to set forth the claims, and challenge critics to refute them — and hold their peace when they cannot.

Adapted from an address to the Land Policy Council, London, The Grosvenor Hotel, May 17, 1998.

---

* *Progress and Poverty*, Book VI, Chp. 2

What Is "Consumption"?

———>◦<———

To consume most goods and services is to eat them up, burn them, wear them out, see them break or rust out or crack or tumble down. But how about land, which is neither created nor destroyed by human beings? Land, as space is not used up.

Does that mean that, economically, it is not consumed? No: to consume it is to preempt its service flow, to occupy it for a time-slot, which may be as brief as beating a red light or (rarely) as long as the pyramids last. The other six "Wonders of the Ancient World" have all disappeared without a trace. Relative to land, human works are evanescent. They are gone "Like snow upon the desert's dusty face, lighting a little hour or two." After we are gone, life goes on, on the land once left to us, which we then leave to others. "Time-sharing" was not invented by the vacation condo industry, but is inherent in the nature of land and life.

How do macroeconomists and national income accountants handle that? They don't. It is a great gaping void in conventional theory and public accounting. To handle it explicitly would destroy the theoretical postulate that consumption, defined as "spending on consumer goods," makes jobs.

One can consume land without actually enjoying or occupying it. The essence of consuming land is preempting the time-slot from others. Thus, holding land without using it, or using it below capacity, are forms of wasteful consumption. If you hired a brain surgeon at his usual hourly rate to weed your garden and mow your lawn, economists would recognize it as wasteful consumption — but if you hold onto a $5 million Malibu beachfront to visit twice a year, that's ignored.

Land is reusable. As there is never any new supply, the old has to be (and is) recycled periodically, and will be in perpetuity, without changing form or location. Melded briefly with fixed buildings, land always survives them to go one more round of use. Even while melded with capital, land always is fit for another use, unlike the capital on it. Land value in cities has been defined as "what is left after a good fire." Arsonists have taken that quite literally.

The opportunity cost of capital is fleeting. Capital loses most of it the moment it is committed to a specific form, whose physical alternative use is often mere scrap. Land's "opportunity cost" is real and viable at all times. The scrap value of capital is often zero or negative (as when, for example, the cost of tearing down an obsolete building lowers the price of a parcel of urban real estate).

Capital, once formed, soon withers away unless there is capital recovery enough to return the original amount over economic life, and the capital recovery is reinvested. Capital recovery is cash flow less interest on the unrecovered balance, with the latter always a prior charge.

Capital is kept in existence from age to age not by preservation or permanence but by constant replacement, while land is the place on which generations of capital come and go.

When we speak of land turnover it refers only to ownership turnover, i.e. the percentage of the fixed supply that changes hands each period. There is no real turnover in the sense of wearing-out and replacement. And even the ownership turnover is very slow compared with capital. Capital turns over constantly, in the normal course of production and consumption.

Something like 3-4% of land parcels turn over annually. Larger, high-valued holdings turn over more slowly, so perhaps one or two percent of the land, measured by value, changes hands yearly. On the other hand, the entire inventory of consumable goods changes hands, normally several times a year, in the natural flow of production. A large share of "durable" capital returns half its value within four or five years. Ownership turnover is inherent in physical turnover.

As noted, to consume land economically is merely to preempt a time-slot from others, regardless of what one does with it. The unreaped harvests of idle land flow down the river and out the gates of time like water wasting through a desert. Lost water may sometimes be useful downstream; lost time never returns. To keep others from using a time-slot is to consume it.

The value of preemption is the highest and best use that might have been made of the land preempted. That is the economic cost. The land is not responsible if the manager fails to realize its value at optimal capacity. Neither are the persons who are excluded. Only the preemptor is responsible, as a manager. This person deserves credit for performing above par and blame for falling below.

A great deal of land in fact is not allocated to its highest and best use. The shortfall of realized ground rent below potential ground rent is properly a debit to the manager's account, not the land's — and the party responsible for the manager is the holder of title.

Most economic theorizing has failed to bring out this point. The tendency is to treat ground rent as a residual, a waste basket for all the errors and dereliction of responsible economic actors. This has resulted in greatly understating the value of land relative to other factors of production. Institutional and social factors, too, often obscure the opportunity cost of land.

Theorizing has been slow to recognize facts that are obvious in practice. In dividing value between land and a building affixed to it, the standard practice of appraisers, and speculative buyers too, is the "building-residual method." The land is appraised as though it were vacant; any remaining real estate value is assigned to the building. The building, once attached to a specific site, loses the mobility of place and form that fluid capital possesses, and has no opportunity cost but scrap value, often negative. Land, always lacking mobility of place, retains mobility of reuse because of its versatility, permanence, and irreproduceable location.

To repeat: though land does not get used up, it *does* get consumed, by title-holders who preempt a time-slot of space. That has the most profound implications for the meaning of "consumption" in economic thinking, and "consumer taxation" in fiscal policy. Economists have neglected and papered over these matters almost completely. Let us pursue the point.

How shall we measure land-consumption by owners, where no rent is paid? Is it purely subjective? Does it vary with the owner's mood and health? It is simpler than that, and fully practicable. The measure is the market opportunity cost of land, e.g. the price times the interest rate. Holding an urban site has been likened to holding a reserved seat at a play, ballgame, or concert. The seat-holder properly helps pay for the event, whether or not there to enjoy it. As a result, very few paid customers fail to show up. Likewise, people who pay cash rent for land seldom leave it vacant. Doubtless if people paid regular cash taxes to hold land, they, too, would consume (preempt) less.

Proponents of "consumer taxation" almost universally overlook this point. I am not aware of one who has proposed including land-consumption in the tax base. Aaron and Galper[*], propounding a "cash-flow tax," explicitly allow for letting each succeeding owner expense land purchase, effectively exempting land rents from taxation 100%. So do Hall and Rabushka[†] in their "Bible" on the flat tax, and so do most current agitators for a national sales tax or VAT.

So-called consumer taxes actually imposed now and in the past bear heavily on the necessities of median and poor families. We deride the salt tax of the French *ancien regime*, and of pre-Gandhian

---

[*] See Aaron, Henry and Galper, Harvey, *Assessing Tax Reform,* 1985, Brookings Institution
[†] See Hall, Robert and Rabushka, Alvin, *The Flat Tax*, 2007, Hoover Institute

India. We recognize them as instruments of tyranny and class warfare, even as we tolerate modern legislators who impose comparable burdens on us, and economists who rationalize such taxes by belittling the necessities of life.

Doing so, they compound the deception in the label "consumer taxation." Much of what is taxed in the name of taxing consumers is actually used for another kind of capital formation. This is what the puritans of early Plymouth called "Inward Wealth" — modern economists call it "human capital." The same economists who say human beings are or contain capital, and we need more of it, turn around and tell us to tax the formation and maintenance of such capital, by calling it "consumption." Coupling this with their proposed exemption of land-consumption we have the ultimate victory and application of semantic cleansing. Inconsistency, thy name is Neoclassical Economist!

Leading modern philosophers of fostering "human capital," like Gary Becker and Theodore Schultz, think of it as post-graduate education, which happens to be their profession. Logically, though, it should include undergraduate education, and secondary education before that, primary before that, and why stop there? Parenting is part of education. Before that comes conception; before that (usually), marriage; before that, courtship; and so on. There is no logical stopping point, back to Adam and Eve. That leads us to realize that much, perhaps most of what sales-taxers stigmatize and down-value as "consumption" is actually human capital formation.

Bottom line? To tax consumption properly we should tax all land held for housing above some reasonable minimum needed for health and children; all land held for recreation; and all land held without using it at all. And we should NOT tax most of what economists today carelessly call "consumption."

Groundswell, *October 2005*

Rent-Seeking
and Global Conflict

ational governments originate historically to acquire, hold and police land. Other functions are assumed later, but sovereignty over land is always the first business. Private parties hold land from the sovereign: every chain of title goes back to a grantor who originally seized the land.

When economists today speak of "rent-seeking" they usually are thinking not of basic land rent. "Rent-seeking" is considered in subtle and sophisticated terms, looking at dribs and drabs of transfer rent derived from contracting advantages. They develop abstract models for gaming optimally with imperfect information, and so on. By emphasizing the arcane while ignoring the basic they resemble the proverbial expert who fine-tunes all the details and elaborations as he forges on to the grand disaster.

Indeed, we have had one such disaster. Viet Nam was viewed by many as an economists' war, rationally planned and led by the best and the brightest systems analysts, exemplified by Robert McNamara, the brilliant, energetic Secretary of Defense. One should not be surprised at the post-Viet Nam decline of interest in applying modern economic theory to questions of global conflict. We economists would be more useful to statesmen if we looked first at rent-seeking in the grosser sense of "land-grabbing," where the whole bundle is at stake. When William of Normandy conquered England the prize was land rent, all of it. He and his retainers dispossessed the local rent-collectors. It was simple, gross, and basic, and much more consequential than the trivial rent-seeking we model today. The bulk of the natives may have been affected only marginally: they just paid Lord B instead of Lord A. But it made all the difference to Lords B and A, the ones who made basic decisions about global conflict and cooperation.

Again, from the 17th century Europeans invaded North America, dispossessed the natives and each other, until today we pay our daily rent for a little slice of land which has been won and kept by a long chain of wars.

The roof over our heads is different. It is the product of capital formation. Someone saved from income, and paid workers to construct the building. Its present value is lowered by depreciation and obsolescence, so it is rentable today mainly for its appreciated site — to which therefore an economist or an appraiser must impute most of the real estate's market value.

The site *per se* was never, nor could ever be the product of capital formation. It pre-existed man, who could only acquire it by taking. It is fair to say that throughout most of history that is what warfare was about, seizing and holding and policing land. This is not to deny ancillary causes and issues of war, such as disputing the pathway to Heaven, ethnic pride, paranoia, or a leader's need to divert people from domestic problems. Neither is this to deny that territorial expansion is often (economically) self-defeating. Many empires, probably most, cost more than they return, a discovery that accounts for the well-being of small nations like Sweden, Austria, Denmark and The Netherlands, which gained by abandoning destiny and empire. Nevertheless: however much the whole imperial nation loses, certain parties gain — and it is they who promote and sustain aggressive behavior.

Economists conventionally bury this point when they submit that "national defense is a public good." Is it?

"Defense" is a loaded word which rationalizes as it describes. "Military spending" is more neutral, and will be used here. It is worth remembering that the German *Schutz* (as in *Schutz-Staffel*) and *Wehr* (as in *Wehrmacht*) both translate as "defense." *Lebensraum* (literally, "living space") is a more forthright term, and explains much more about Nazi aggressions.

To call something a "public good" is to say that all gain from it equally. But that is not true even of pure defense proper. What is defended behind the defense wall is land previously seized. The Lords and Barons have much at stake; the serfs and vagrants very little. Rent is what is being defended, along with, no doubt, traditional feelings of *machismo* and some local folkways and mores.

Wages, as well as the return for capital formation, ultimately need little defense because they are economically functional. They are paid for real service and sacrifices, and will command a return in any viable system. Labor is also more migratory. "Fixed" capital also migrates economically, as capital recovery funds are reinvested elsewhere. Land, in contrast, does not migrate among nations. Nations are defined as areas of land.

However, it is outside the defense wall of the nation proper that rent-seeking is most dynamic and destabilizing. Military force (often in tandem with finance) is used to project sovereignty into foreign nations, and over no-man's-lands like the oceans, polar regions, radio spectrum, and outer space. Offshore rent-seekers are of two general kinds.

1. "Caciques." This is a generic term for local cooperating rulers from the native population. It is more neutral than Quisling, and most caciques are more independent than he was.[*] Imperial metropolitan powers normally work through caciques. Turnover among individual caciques is sometimes high, but they are drawn from the matrix of the local landholding oligarchy which is

---

[*] Vidkun Abraham Lauritz Jonssøn Quisling was a Norweigian politician who seized power in a Nazi-backed coup in 1940; his name became a generic term for a collaborator with an enemy.

quite stable, often thanks to our support.

We relieve the caciques of collecting and/or paying taxes for their own military, which often double as domestic police as well. The life of some caciques is risky, but the rewards to caciques and local landholders are often very high. The Sultan of Brunei is the richest man in the world; the extravagance of Ferdinand and Imelda Marcos was legendary.

Unit land values in Tokyo, in its 1980s boom, exceeded those in New York and Chicago by a factor of about ten. One reason (of several) for the difference is that New York and Chicago pay taxes to defend Tokyo, along with what the Japanese once called the Greater East Asia Co-Prosperity Sphere. Roosevelt in 1941 stopped Japan at Viet Nam, precipitating Pearl Harbor. But Eisenhower said in 1959 we must defend Viet Nam to protect the Japanese resource base.

2. US or allied multinational interests, mostly corporations. The cacique is expected to assign to them, or be complaisant in their taking, concessions and resources like minerals, transportation routes, communications, bank charters, plantations, etc. Natives normally control more of the traditional resources like farmland. Foreigners specialize more in less visible, more novel and sophisticated resources like undiscovered minerals (exploration rights), navigation rights, radio spectrum, overflights, bank charters, etc.

Both these groups have the acutest incentive to influence US policies, and large discretionary funds at hand. Therefore they tend to dominate US statecraft. The US government is probably more vulnerable to such foreign influence than most, because of our size and weakly developed sense of honorable dedication to the national interest. The English once terminated a dynasty, the Stuarts, which was caught taking support from France; but Americans hardly notice when retired Congressmen take work lobbying for foreign sugar producers, etc.

Self-evidently, rivalry to appropriate limited rent-yielding resources must lead to conflict. It has to, because land is not produced, nor stored up like capital by saving. Modern economics glosses over this by stressing that land, like other resources, is allocated by the market. That may be, but *distribution* is something else. Every land title in the world goes back to a taking by force.

It will be objected that one can buy in peacefully once a tenure is firmly established, with alienable titles. There is certainly no intent to deny this. The problem is that a successor-in-interest stands on no firmer footing than the original. There is no laundering: every landholder can consult his chain of title and see how it originated. Indeed, it has been said that those who buy stolen property are the chief cause of crime. Fencing itself is a crime. However one may side on that question, it helps account for the extreme alarm of US statecraft toward any foreign country, however weak and innocuous, which expropriates any such successor-in-interest. Demonstration effects are contagious and threatening. The defensiveness of the insecure is a major cause of global conflict.

More destabilizing yet is the ambitious rent-seeker offshore, who finds his biggest gains in the riskiest ways, ways that unfortunately impose high risks on the US. The biggest gains to rent-seekers come from buying in on the ground floor, cheap, when tenures are precarious or uncertain.

Then one invokes the US armed forces and the sanctions of ancillary statecraft to raise the value of one's acquisition. The three main concerns are to firm up precarious tenures (as by supporting the government that granted them); to hold down taxes (as by lending the US armed forces); and to avoid pure competition (as by giving preferential access to the US market, or Pentagon procurers).

There have been spectacular success stories. Aramco is one. It originated in 1933 with a capital of $100,000. By 1970 it was valued at well over $5 billion. Of course that increase might represent accumulated capital flows from the US owners; but such was not the fact.

There are four sources of value of foreign holdings: capital flows, plowbacks, appropriations, and appreciation. In many cases like Aramco the last two far outweigh the first. But they are products of statecraft and force, not of capital inputs proper.

Tenure granted by unstable governments is not worth much, and is therefore cheap to acquire. In 1960, for example, Patrice Lumumba pledged a substantial share of the Congo in return for a relatively modest loan from a Wall Street financier.

Of course there are also failures and losses, and someone might even try to show that aggregate losses exceed aggregate gains. But Adam Smith observed long ago that when an occupation offers a small number of extremely high rewards, its attractiveness is enhanced out of all proportion to their aggregate value. It is not just the successes, but all the attempts that provoke global conflict.

We are trained and conditioned to think of land tenure as something stable and inherited, with secure roots in history. In fact, that which was inherited can never be taken as given unless the origins bear examination. Past appropriation invites future expropriation. One result of that is a legal system even in "capitalist" America which tolerates rather extreme invasions of land value through zoning, rent control, taxation, and field price controls, without there being a legal "taking" such as might be prohibited by the 5th and 14th Amendments.

But in addition, tenure is constantly being created at the interfaces among sovereignties. Each is a potential flashpoint. Title to land is also contested within many sovereignties, like Mexico 1910-40, and Cuba 1962. Current examples are also nearby in Guatemala, El Salvador and Nicaragua. Every such internal contest makes an international incident or crisis.

Tenure is created at the margins of settlement and/or exploration, as on Alaska's Outer Continental Shelf; the margins of political stability; and the margins of research and technology. In addition, tenure is constantly being tightened and refined at higher levels of intensity and demand for the services of scarce land. In recent decades the unprecedented voracious resource demands of the United States have been a major dynamic.

These views have been characterized by some as "Marxist," because of the explicit recognition of special class interests. If this be Marxism make the most of it; the point, if any, is *ad hominem*. But the views here differ from Marx's. For one, Marx was an under-consumptionist who attributed imperialism to a search for overseas markets, not rent-seeking. For another, Marx made no sharp consistent distinction between land and capital.

The present views point toward specific policy changes. To minimize global conflict, a nation should use its tax system to recoup rents from beneficiaries of its statecraft. This would deflate the rent-seeking incentive to provocative behavior, as well as the discretionary funds used to gain political support. There is little gain to the nation as a whole — and high cost — in creating rents for a few individuals or corporations. A surtax on income from foreign sources, for example, rather than the present preferential treatment, is indicated.

An analogous movement is already underway in municipal affairs. Robert Freilich, a lawyer sometimes called the "father of growth control," has worked out systems of urban growth whereby newly annexed lands must pay the full costs of their own development, instead of leeching on central cities as has been the custom. This has, where applied, drastically cooled down the passion for leapfrog annexations. I trust the analogy between municipal and national imperialism is evident.

To strengthen the nation and move toward justifying labeling defense a "public good," there must be a wider sharing of rents. This is a simple matter of readjusting tax systems. Many oil-rich jurisdictions already provide models, albeit modest in degree (like Alaska's social dividend from oil royalties). Canada has a partially-developed system of interprovincial equalization of resource revenues. The result there, as one might expect, has been to heighten the sense of national unity and patriotism in the constructive sense, increasing the numbers of citizens honorably devoted to the nation as such.

Summary for a University of California seminar on Global Conflict and Cooperation, Laguna Beach, February, 1988

The Philippines: Land Reform through Tax Reform

A fossilized economy

We American GIs, ca. 1945, thought we were badly fed —
but local children were salvaging our garbage. *"C'est la guerre,"* we
explained — easy answer. Seventy-five years later, the poverty and
degradation remain, while the rest of Southeast Asia is dynamic. Now we see, *"Ce n'est pas la guerre: c'est la propriété foncière"* —
property in land. What I saw then, in essence, is what one still sees
today:

The Philippine economy is truly colonial, with plantation
agriculture on the best lands. Plantations are economically sterile,
generating no creative towns and cities to serve local agriculture.
This was the case, for example, in the ante-bellum south, USA, in
contrast to ante-bellum New England. Or compare the west side
of California's San Joaquin Valley with the east side, with its many
small cities. Philippine latifundia leads to marked contrasts of intensity of land use: the fertile lowlands around Tarlac are underused;
marginal hill-lands (Ilocos, Baguio) are overcrowded.

This is a class society, without concealment or apology. I drive
my mess-boy to his barrio to see his sick mother, and he anxious-
ly demands we must check in with a person whom the mess-boy

insists on calling "The Spanish Master," a Spanish citizen with plans to return to Spain and marry after age 40. Meantime, he has a special claim on virgins of the barrio; for, as Henry George put it, "to own the land is to own the people." Complexions of children on the terrace suggest he does not study planned parenthood.

Appropriate courtship mores as seen by middle-class American GIs: girls who can afford not being prostitutes adopt Spanish puritanism, "no-touch." It's one or the other.

Manila, "Pearl of the Orient," is where absentee owners live and spend their rents. It is a sterile city, generating little industry. Commerce thrives mainly in foreign enclaves.

Foreign domination

There are many reasons why the Philippines were easy prey for foreign intervention. Seven thousand islands are vulnerable to marine invasion. Major world naval powers covet the harbors. The indigenous people spoke more than a hundred dialects, and had many quarrels. This made it easier for native religions to yield to Spanish missionaries or, on the southern island of Mindanao, Muslims.

Even Magellan was tempted: he was killed interceding in a native quarrel. Unfortunately for the Filipinos, later Spaniards survived better. Spanish missionaries founded Manila, and spread out. Spanish Puritanism and the chivalric conscience created a need for a persuasive hypocrisy to rationalize exploitative imperialism. To the rescue: the *Encomienda*, a colonizing institution blending three imperialisms: cultural, military and economic. It made natives pay rent to finance their own suppression — and their instruction in The Faith. Recall the sardonic chorus from *Man of La Mancha:* "We were only thinking of them."

Lands were granted by Spanish Kings (as were the California missions). In 1898 America succeeded Spain as governor of the islands, but the Treaty of Paris of that year validated the private and ecclesiastical land titles stemming from Spanish kings of centuries past. (The same thing had happened in California after the Treaty of

Guadelupe-Hidalgo, 1848. Imperial powers everywhere had learned it is much easier to win empires by coopting the local landowners in this way.) Undisturbed, *encomiendas* ripen into fee simple titles. With social and military tax obligations reduced, the land titles rise in value. Those sly Spaniards, to let us "win"!

The Filipino leader Emilio Aguinaldo, our ally against Spain, pressed for independence. This might have led to nationalization of large estates, in which America's rich and powerful already had major interests, but probably not, since Aguinaldo was more interested in nationalism and power than in radical reforms. The American military nonetheless invaded (1898) to suppress Aguinaldo in a bloody war, followed by indefinite occupation. The American "savior" became the new oppressor.

For the next four decades (the US relinquished *de jure* sovereignty over the Philippines in 1946), the Philippines was a field and training ground for American men on horseback, with repressive, anti-democratic attitudes which they then brought home: Frederick Funston; Leonard Wood; Henry L. Stimson; Douglas MacArthur — men for whom we name boulevards and forts. Leonard Wood, little remembered today, spent the 1910-20 decade in the US drumming up support for a military draft — an instrument of power for President Woodrow Wilson. After the war Republican Wood allied with Democratic A.G. Mitchell Palmer and his police chief, J. Edgar Hoover, to deport labor leaders whom he considered radical. Both Wood and Palmer aspired to the presidential nominations of their respective Parties, on extreme rightwing programs, and Wood almost made it.

The price of power is that Washington is besieged by foreign lobbyists, a corrupting influence. Sugar lobbyists are among the worst. The chief Filipino lobbyist in US was Manuel Quezon. Washington picked him as its chosen instrument, or cacique. Quezon moved the capital to an eponymous private estate outside Manila.

During the Japanese occupation, Spanish titles were undisturbed. Spain was almost, if not quite, one of the Axis Powers,

Franco being under the wing of Hitler and Mussolini. All-out war is just for soldiers, the cannon fodder, while the unwritten transnational comity of property protects landholders. The last time the US confiscated lands from the losers was during and after the American Revolution, and that was done by local militiamen and colonial governments. Hamilton, dominating the US Government from 1789-1801, tried his best to compensate the evicted Tories, but lacked the tax revenues and the power.

Under Philippine "independence," after 1946, land titles of Spanish collaborators were undisturbed. Priority went to putting down the Hukbalahaps, native rebels organized and indoctrinated by communists. The Huks made a handy bogeyman for the *rentiers* to use to justify forcible repression of all land reformers. In 1972, the Huk problem was still unresolved, so Marcos declared martial law. In 1986 the US engineered the Aquino presidency, again promising land reform.

It still hasn't happened. Corazón Aquino emerged as just another political hypocrite who promised reform but backed off from her window of opportunity, and passed the buck to an unwilling Congress. US presence manifests the "Cacique" syndrome: US pays for defense, so they needn't tax themselves. This is landlordship in its purest form, free even of military obligations. The Philippine Army focuses on suppressing Filipinos, making them pay rent.

Role of the Church

The Roman Catholic Church was totally implicated in the Spanish conquest, just as Protestant Yale missionaries were in the conquest of Hawaii. *Encomienda* financed cultural conquest, conversion and submission. Jesuits also acquired vast lands in the 19th century. We surmise that the clergy restrained the worst excesses of landholders, as today — but offered no preventive therapy. Do those who bind up wounds develop a vested interest in wounds? Dom Hélder Pessoa Câmara, the Brazilian Archbishop, learned the hard way how the establishment circumscribed his role: "I helped the poor and they called me a saint; I ask why they are poor and they call me a communist."

José Rizal was the foremost martyr of the struggle for independence from Spain. Unlike too many Filipino rebel leaders he was intellectual, spiritual, and incorruptible. He wrote books attacking religious orders, which he identified with the status quo of maldistribution of land; he was convicted of rebellion, sedition and conspiracy, and executed in 1896 by the Spanish army.

The upper Catholic hierarchy has generally supported the prevailing land dispensation and system. Liberal popes criticize the worst abuses and their indirect results (like poverty, unemployment and death squads) but uphold the core concept of private collection of rents and unearned increments. There is a centuries-long tradition of church as major landholder.

When Lyndon Johnson was waging his "War on Poverty," Cardinal Spellman of New York used his power and influence to divert him into helping to suppress landless peasants fighting French landlords in Viet Nam. There was an attempt to kill Paul VI in Manila, 1970. When Latin American clerics like Boff and Gutierrez promoted "Liberation Theology," Pope John Paul II suppressed them. His leading spokesman, Cardinal Ratzinger, succeeded him as Pope and continued to muffle the Liberationists.

Can the Church be changed? There is change in the field, among brave and dedicated priests on the firing line, but it is poorly supported at the top, and vulnerable to local bravos in the field. Philippine society needs radical, wrenching reforms. But the church, trying to be liberal, has lost its radical mission. Trying to conciliate, the church has not led. Trying to participate, the church has been coopted. Trying to make religion easy, the church has made it trivial.

Role of the United States

The Pentagon wants bases: Cavite, Subic, Clark Field, etc. The rationale of imperialism is ever circular, *petitio principii:* the function of each base is to support the others, and vice versa. None dare call it imperialism — by asking why have the whole regional presence in the first place. There is oil in the South China Sea; maybe someday Manila will be leasing some of it. But on the whole, there are no strategic resource benefits to justify the cost of our military spending. Sugar and rice add to our surpluses.

Why are we there? There were few prior US holdings in 1898, when Adm. Dewey said "You may fire when ready, Gridley." A more general answer is that there were "potential absentees," the sort who grabbed Hawaii about the same time, following the imperialist formula: get land cheap, then call the Marines to firm up precarious tenures and get preferential political treatment. Henry L. Stimson, a Skull-and-Bones Yale man with prior service in Nicaragua, was no stranger to this formula; his protégé McGeorge Bundy also tried it later in Viet Nam.

What kind of preferential treatment? Putting down Aguinaldo firmed up land tenures. After that, land is worth more with preferential access to the US sugar market. Sugar is a favorite enterprise for absentee landholders because it needs lots of land with little labor or management.

Land is worth more if you get police protection without paying taxes. There is direct US aid, as well as loans and grants and base rentals and Pentagon spending, and the shelter of US forces. Result? Little pressure on holders of Philippine land to pay taxes, direct or otherwise. That has long been the essential formula of would-be world hegemons: turn the local gentry into caciques' zamindars.

Ironically, it is now proposed that US taxpayers finance Philippine land reform by buying back the same land their spending makes valuable, to return to the Filipinos from whom it was stolen. Who lost the Spanish-American War? The American taxpayer seems to be the ultimate patsy. His sons may win battles, but his brains are hors de combat.

He is fed on The Great Secular Superstition that unearned income and stolen property are sacred, and protecting them is an obligation owed to God and country. He holds it a moral and social lapse to challenge The Superstition, which he wraps in the flag, democracy, freedom, church and country — to hide its nakedness.

An occasional American does, to be sure, preach land reform. There was Robert Hardie, 1952, fresh from the heady success of reshaping Japan under MacArthur, then with STEM of MSA. But Hardie was expelled, his report recalled and suppressed under Quirino.

Adm. Raymond Spruance, US Ambassador, 1952-55, was a believer in Henry George. As hero of Midway Island, he dealt from some strength. Demonstration effects spilled over from Japan and Taiwan. Land Reform was popular with personnel at the UN, World Bank, IMF, etc. Charismatic, popular President Ramon Magsaysay, 1953-57, was dedicated to land reform. But Spruance, appointed by Harry Truman, was quickly made a lame duck by another military hero, President Eisenhower. It was also the sick and sinister age of Joseph McCarthy and Edward Lansdale, who prevailed. Land reform was equated with Communism, and suppressed.

Role of Philippine Nationalism

Dr. Sun Yat-sen's classic testament, the San Min Chu I, enunciated three principles to guide governance in the new China: nationalism, democracy and "right livelihood," which meant a Georgist tax system. Sun had been exposed to Henry George's ideas while living in Hawaii, and of course then found ample precedents in Chinese history.

Nationalism has a bad odor for its abuses, and yet every egalitarian polity we know is national. Philippine nationalism is underdeveloped. The sentiment and rhetoric are there, but in practice, the US defends their shores, rents their bases, suppresses their rebels, buys their exports, obviates their taxes — who needs nationalism? A shell of nationalism has developed, nonetheless. Natural resources "belong to the state." Exploitation is limited to citizens, or corporations 60% citizen-owned. Florid, pompous language abounds in official documents. It is the language of hypocrisy. *De facto* and *de jure* are far apart. The same is true in British Columbia, 95% owned by the Crown Provincial but leased on easy terms to MacMillan Bloedel et al. Likewise, California's state constitution alleges that water rights in California are owned by "the people."

Role of Filipino-Americans

Although they have the most direct human interest, Filipino-Americans are rarely consulted in making US policy. They might lead, finance and give reasonable direction to reform, as Irish-Americans once did. Filipino-Americans could do an even better job. Unfortunately, however, although Filipinos are the second fastest-growing stream of immigrants, after Koreans, they are nearly invisible. In Los Angeles, there are 2.5 times as many Philippine natives as Japanese natives, but who knows where to find Little Manila? In the Bay Area, Filipino-Americans cluster along Stockton Street, below Grant Avenue, and in the cities of Stockton and Daly City. But Stockton just went bankrupt, while Daly City, at the Southwest end of the BART system, has a dead look.

Why are Filipino-Americans invisible and powerless? a) They are below a critical mass (there may be an explosion when they reach it). b) They have no distinctive church; instead they melt in with other Catholics, who are settled and conservative. c) They have only a weak entrepreneurial tradition and class, like African-Americans. d) They are poor — which intensifies and magnifies the first three.

Should reformers help organize and motivate this group? Earlier Irish experience gives pause. Ethnic groups are just that, and later fall away from reform as such. The cases of Parnell, Corrigan, Ford, Powderly, Croker, and other Irish-Americans illustrate the tendency. Are Jewish-Americans going the same route? Israel was founded and led by idealistic Jews who set up *kibbutzim* to divide land equally, but on Israel's 50-year Jubilee the new leaders never mentioned the true meaning of Jubilee.

What can Americans do?

We can start by reducing American support, in reasonable stages but with firm direction and sustained resolution. Filipinos can defend their own nation, if they:

a) Tax their own lands, especially the absentees;

b) Placate dissident populations (let *their* fear of Marxism drive them, not ours);

c) Foster development at home, following Japan, Taiwan, Singapore, Korea, Hong Kong.

We must give up our illusions of cultural superiority, and of control. It may, sometimes, under great pressure, be possible to impose a better system on an occupied nation than it would produce itself: Hong Kong and Singapore may be examples. But the greatest examples of "economic development" have been home-grown. The Philippines have their own Congress, firmly controlled by Philippine landholders, whose power derives from their long history of collaboration with occupying foreigners like ourselves.

Foreign aid should be limited to one kind alone: technical assistance assessing land, avoiding regressive assessment, and collecting taxes based on market value of land. Philippine tax administration is advanced enough to benefit from aid, and backward and corrupt enough to need it.

Tax reform of this kind obviates other land reform, because the market reforms itself under this stimulus. This is a bold, bare, enormous fact that is almost universally obscured and misunderstood. The landholder is the successor-in-interest to those who stole the land from the majority. He compensates them in three ways: by supporting government; by hiring workers to put the land to its highest use; and by producing goods for the workers to buy with their new wages. The economically sterile plantation system can no longer support itself. Supply-side and demand-side economics work together to raise real output and income.

Land reform of this kind is free of the defects that have made most other land reforms exercises in mere tokenism, stalling, graft and CIA militarism. Land value taxation raises money, without burdening any useful activity. Liberal "land reform" buyouts cost money — raised, if at all, by taxing commerce, industry and labor in the cities and aborting urban development, the very thing this country needs most.

Neo-Liberal "land reform" benefits at best the handful of lucky ones who get farms; land taxation helps everyone by lowering other taxes, making jobs and increasing output. Neo-Liberal "land reform" accepts and validates the extreme concentration of wealth that curses the Philippines; land taxation strikes its root. Neo-Liberal "land reform" is mostly agrarian; land taxation deals with urban, mineral, forest and other lands and, properly construed, deals with all economic land including fisheries, radio spectrum, air rights, water rights, amenity rights, recreational values, etc.

Of course, the very virtues of land value taxation guarantee it will arouse powerful opposition. Greed and fear often have their way; it was ever thus. But let that be their problem, not ours: no reason for us to be bamboozled or deterred.

Finally, if we advocate real, meaningful land reform as described here, we must reject hypocrisy and stalling, expressed in vague words without specific procedures for implementation. Don't believe that "all natural resources belong to the people" just because "that's what it says here."

Also, we should avoid touting free trade in colonial settings. It has become a code-word of Spanish-Master types for a land-using, unbalanced, labor-evicting, foreign-enclave sterile economy (cf. the ante-bellum cotton South). Rather, settle the land (including urban land), by collecting its rent for public revenue, and free trade will flourish — as in Taiwan.

Is it too late?

A century ago, Henry George wielded great influence. How did he do it? First he allied with radical rebels, 1879-86. Only thus did he develop power to frighten landholders and become worth coopting. Was cooptation death? No, it was a golden age of constructive reform in America, 1886-1917, the Progressive Era. First you rebel, then ally, to have real impact. It is a dynamic process, however, and must be repeated regularly because each cycle ends in decadence. It's time to begin again. What can honest people do now? They can combat The Great Secular Superstition in schools and churches, move into influential positions in the screening processes that generate ideas and select leaders. They can keep their faith by continuing association and good will.

Adapted from an address to the World Affairs Council,
San Francisco, October 1987

Repopulating New Orleans

Our latest Nobelist in economics, Professor Thomas Schelling, offerred the following advice about New Orleans: "There is no market solution to New Orleans. It is essentially a problem of coordinating expectations...." By that he meant simply that each person's incentive to return home and rebuild depends on his or her confidence that others will do likewise. There must be "credible commitments," Schelling said. "But achieving this coordination in the circumstances of New Orleans seems impossible.... There are classes of problems that free markets simply do not deal with well. If ever there was an example, the rebuilding of New Orleans is it."

So economics has come to this. Schelling is a specialist in "complex market behavior using game theory." His current book is *Strategies of Commitment*. A reviewer praises him as one who "takes on practical questions." Apparently practical New Orleans is too complex for the most advanced modern theory. Only yesterday, the approved professional posture was not to recommend programs, but just advise timidly on how different ones might work, covering one's back with caveats. Now our top dog has gone the next step, and advises us that nothing can work, not even the market. A discipline with roots in Utilitarianism has morphed into Futilitarianism. Accordingly, "prestigious" graduate schools mill out neutered clones — we see them in the job market at this time every year — with templates and powerpoints for everything, and solutions for nothing.

Actually, there is a time-tested way to solve the problem that defeats Schelling and his "game theory." American urban settlers and investors have a long history of building cities by "coordinating expectations." In 1891 the traveling Lord James Bryce noted of Americans, "Men seem to live in the future rather than in the present... they see the country not merely as it is, but as it will be...." They achieved critical urban mass by faith in each other's intentions.

The mutual faith was economic more than theological. Bryce noted that in 1891 "State revenue is almost wholly direct, because of the commerce clause." The commerce clause blocked states from taxing imports, the major alternative to taxing property. And so "The chief tax is in every State (and locality) a property tax...." This property tax at that time fell mostly on land values, because that is most of what there was to tax. This was the mechanism for "coordinating expectations." Each landowner felt the pressure to use his land, knowing his neighbors felt the same pressure at the same time. (There were also pioneering religious and ethnic groups that fostered mutual faith, as the Greek Orthodox community is doing now in its small part of New Orleans. In "game theory" we are all greedy monads, so such things do not happen in the models.)

It's not that Schelling never heard of the stimulative effect of taxing land values. In 1971 I had the privilege of presenting it to a seminar at the Brookings Institution. I suggested raising the land tax, and lowering sales taxes, and taxes on buildings. Most attendees participated with at least mild sympathy, notably excepting Thomas Schelling. He objected that any change in tax policy would break the social contract, destabilize expectations, shatter investor confidence, and risk bringing the world down in ruins.

A year earlier I had spoken on the same point to a New Orleans civic group that sponsored a Brookings urbanism program. They were charming hosts, eager for ideas to clear "undesirable" neighborhoods, but obsessed with preserving *Le Vieux Carré* (the French Quarter) which they saw as unique, interdependent, wholesome, a money machine, and too fragile to survive competition that would replace it with the commonplace. Like Schelling, they chose stasis, with the results that we see today. Actually, there can be no stasis: buildings depreciate every year, and need constant upkeep, operation, adaptation to markets, and often replacement.

New Orleans also has a clutch of private universities where abstract thoughts soar into the rare, without relieving the commonplace squalor around them, any more than Yale, Columbia, Chicago, Penn, MIT, Duke, Marquette, Howard, Catholic, Hopkins, or USC uplift their respective neighborhoods. Tulane has long been the nursling of New Orleans's old power elite, and nursery of the new. Loyola has selected an extremist among extremist libertarians, Walter Block, for a distinguished named professorship. We are still waiting for some New Orleans professors to tell us how to save the City they serve.

A going city or region, destroyed by catastrophe, has an easier time returning to critical mass than does a new city or region flying blind. London renewed itself after the Great Fire of 1666; Northern New England after being ravaged in King Philip's War, 1675-76; Schenectady after Frontenac razed it in 1690; Lisbon after the quake of 1755; Dutch cities after flooding themselves out to balk successive Spanish, French, and German invaders; Moscow after 1812; and Washington, D.C., after 1813. In 1848, John Stuart Mill made a major point in his *Principles* on "the great rapidity with which countries recover from a state of devastation; the disappearance, in a short time, of all traces of the mischiefs done by earthquakes, floods, hurricanes, and the ravages of war." Since Mill there have been a series of such rebirths: Atlanta after Sherman; Chicago after 1871; swaths of Wisconsin after the epic 1871 fire named for little Peshtigo; Johnstown, PA, after its killer flood of 1889; San Francisco after its quake and fire of 1906; Flanders after World War I; Ventura County, California, after the St. Francis dam disaster; Tokyo after 1926; Nanking after Japan's soldiers raped it. After World War II came Germany's *Wirtschaftswunder*, and rebuilding of

Coventry, Rotterdam, Tokyo again, Hiroshima, Nagasaki, much of Russia, Anchorage after its quake, Kobe after its, and so on, and on.

Historian Alexander Gerschenkron popularized the "advantage of a late start" in industrial competition. Destruction provides that advantage: wipe out the obsolescent and depreciated old capital and the renewed city will embody the latest technology in its capital. The rioters and arsonists of 1967 boasted with some justice that they were doing "instant urban renewal." Burning and razing releases a vast and seasoned land area for the new. It couples the advantage of a late start with the forward inertia of an early start. We rightly deplore the human cost and suffering of such wild violence. It is better to adopt the kinder, gentler program of tax reform.

Permanent hazards may remain. Yet, Chicago was rebuilt on the foundation of its "stinking swamp," where Chicago architects pioneered the modern skyscraper on deep caissons. Tokyo was rebuilt at the confluence of four tectonic plates, and after 1945 with no navy or army of its own. San Francisco was rebuilt on the San Andreas Fault, and went high-rise on its crazy hills while level Los Angeles was still capping building heights and opting for sprawl. Much of the Netherlands thrives below sea level. Hong Kong grew capitalistically in the jaws of Mao, and Johannesburg amid newly empowered blacks with scores to settle.

After disaster, location remains, and location makes cities. Greater New Orleans was recently the largest port in the world, in tonnage. People, enterprise, and investment also make cities. Herein lies the greater hazard, for many American cities self-destruct without the bang of natural disasters, but with a whimper of futility, like Buffalo, Cincinnati, Detroit, Camden, or East St. Louis. New Orleans today has a kind of dynamism that those decaying cities lack. Demand for its real estate is holding up well, and rising in the unflooded areas like the Gentilly Ridge. Even in the flooded and abandoned areas there is strong demand from absentee speculators looking to hold for a free ride up the price elevator as the efforts of others bring back the neighborhoods. Yet, this kind of dynamism is worse than stasis. These absentee bottom fishers choke out other buyers aiming to commit their lives, to rebuild and reside and occupy and make neighborhoods. As "Each man kills the thing he loves," absentee investors collectively drive away the very people who could make their dreams come true. Many of them have no plans, but are waiting for other people's plans. This sort of "coordinating expectations" leads to collective failure. New Orleans' tax system, tragically, penalizes the builders and spares the free riders.

How did other cities come back? Born-again San Francisco, 1907-30, makes an edifying case study in success. What can it teach New Orleans? It had no State or Federal aids to speak of. The state of California had oil, but didn't even tax it — as Louisiana does. It did have private insurance, but so does New Orleans today. It had no power to tax sales or incomes. It had no lock on Sierra water to sell its neighbors, as now; no finished Panama Canal, as now; no regional monopoly comparable to New Orleans' hold on the vast Mississippi Valley. Unlike rival Los Angeles (whose smog lay in the future) it had cold fog, cold-water beaches, no local fuel, nor semitropical farm products, nor easy mountain passes to the east. Its rail and shipping connections were inferior to the major rail and port and shipbuilding complex in rival Oakland, and even to inland Stockton's. It was hilly; much of its flatter space was landfill, in jeopardy both to liquefaction of soil in another quake, and precarious titles (due to the public trust doctrine). Its great bridges were unbuilt — it was more island than peninsula. It was known for eccentricity, drunken sailors, tong wars, labor strife, racism, vice, vigilantism, and civic scandals. In its hinterland, mining was fading; irrigation barely beginning. Lumbering was far north around Eureka; wine around Napa; deciduous fruit around San Jose. Berkeley had the State University, Sacramento the Capitol, Palo Alto Stanford, Oakland and Alameda the major U.S. Naval supply center. How did a City with so few assets raise funds to repair its broken infrastructure and rise from its ashes? It had only the local property tax, and much of this tax base was burned to the ground. The answer is that it taxed the ground itself, raising money while also kindling a new kind of fire under landowners to get on with it, or get out of the way.

Historians have obsessed over the quake and fire, but blanked out the recovery. We do know, though, that in 1907 San Francisco elected a reform Mayor, Edward Robeson Taylor, with a uniquely relevant background: he had helped Henry George write *Progress and Poverty* in 1879. George, of course, is the one who wrote and campaigned for the cause of raising most revenues from a tax on the value of land, exempting labor and buildings. George, Jr.'s bio of his dad calls Taylor the only one who vetted the entire MS. George's academic biographer, Charles Barker, credits Taylor with adding style and class to the work, and some ideas along with it. Taylor's call for action appears in Book VIII, introducing "The Application of the Remedy." If you had been a partner in writing *Progress and Poverty*, and composed its call for action, and became reform Mayor of a razed city with nothing to tax but land value, what would you do?

Reams are in print about how Henry George was not elected Mayor of New York, but nothing about how his colleague E.R. Taylor *was* elected Mayor of San Francisco. While George was barnstorming New York City and the world, as an outsider, Taylor stayed home and rose quietly to the top as an insider.

In 1907, single-tax was in the air. It was natural and easy to go along with Cleveland (Mayors Tom Johnson and Newton Baker), Detroit (Mayor Hazen Pingree), Toledo (Mayors Samuel Jones and Brand Whitlock), Milwaukee (Victor Berger and Mayor Daniel Hoan), Chicago (Mayor Edward F. Dunne, J.P. Altgeld, Ida Tarbell, Henry D. Lloyd, Louis F. Post, Clarence Darrow, Edgar Lee Masters, Jane Addams, et al.), Vancouver (6-time Mayor Louis Denison "Single-tax" Taylor), Houston (Assessor J.J. Pastoriza), San Diego (Assessor Harris Moody), Edmonton, many smaller cities, and doubtless other big cities yet to be researched, that chose to tax buildings less and land more. It was the Golden Age of American cities when they grew like fury, and also with grace: "The City Beautiful" was the motif, expressed in parks and expositions like San

Francisco's 1915 Panama-Pacific International Exposition.

San Francisco bounced back so fast its population grew by 22%, 1900-10, in the very wake of its destruction; it grew another 22%, 1910-20; and another 25%, 1920-30, becoming the 10th largest American city. It did this without expanding its land base, as rival Los Angeles did; and while providing wide parks and public spaces. Indeed it had to pull back from the treacherous filled-in level lands that had given way in the quake. On its hills and dales it housed, and linked with mass transit, a denser population than any city except the Manhattan Borough of New York. For a sense of its gradients, see the chase scenes from the films *Bullitt* or *Trench Coat*. It is these people and their good works that made San Francisco so famously livable, the cynosure of so many eyes, and gave it the massed economic power later to bridge the Bay and the Golden Gate, grab water from the High Sierra, finance the fabulous growth of intensive irrigated farming in the Central Valley, and become the financial, cultural, and tourism center of the Pacific coast.

Mayor Nagin[*] of New Orleans tells the world that Katrina wiped out most of his tax base, so he is impotent. By contrast, in 1907 Mayor Taylor's Committee on Assessment, Revenue, and Taxation reported sanguinely that revenues were still adequate. How could that be? Because before the quake and fire razed the city, 75% of its real estate tax base was already land value.[†] San Francisco also taxed "personal" (movable) property, but it was much less than real estate, and "secured" by land. The coterminous County and School District used the same tax base. If we saw such a situation today we would say the local people had adopted most of Henry George's single tax program *de facto*, whether or not they said so publicly.

It was a jolt to replace the lost part of the tax base by taxing land value more, but small enough to be doable. This firm tax base also sustained San Francisco's credit to finance the great burst of

---

[*] Ray Nagin, Mayor of New Orleans, 2002-2010

[†] San Fancisco *Municipal Reports, FY 1906 and 1907*, p. 777)

civic works that was to follow. Taylor retired in 1909, but soon laid his hands on James Rolph, who remained Mayor for 19 years, 1911-30, a period of civic unity and public works. "Sunny Jim" Rolph expanded city enterprise into water supply, planning, municipally owned mass transit, the Panama-Pacific International Exposition, and the matchless Civic Center. S.F. supplemented the property tax by levying special assessments on land values enhanced by public works like the Stockton Street and Twin Peaks Tunnels. Good fiscal policy did not turn all the knaves into saints, as Gray Brechin has documented in *Imperial San Francisco*. Rolph burned out after 1918 or so, and fell into bad company with venal bankers and imperialist engineers. But San Francisco still rose and throve.

New Orleans has its own special problem, sited below the Mississippi River and its levees. Milton Friedman and his like-thinkers proclaim that markets have solutions for everything that governments botch. Building levees, however, demands cooperation guided by some overall authority, which is what governments are for. A levee protects the land behind it only by shunting water onto other lands, which then require their own levees to shunt the water back, and downstream, and even, as it turned out, upstream. Competition among levee-builders is no panacea, but an endless vicious spiral or "positive feedback loop." Over a century it has led step-by-step to levees four stories high. At one time some engineers, spurred on by ambitious local levee districts, thought that such levees would cause the River to scour its bed and sink down, but the opposite has occurred.

Analytically, the problem is analogous to that of rivals pumping water or oil from a common pool; or fishermen competing to take fish from a finite fishery. In those other contexts, private-property fanatics (i.e., most modern economists) see a "tragedy of the commons" and prescribe privatization, an idea that fits their doctrinaire thinking as comfortably as an old shoe. Levees, however, are there to protect lands already private, and that calls for different thinking.

Since the Mississippi watershed covers half the country, the central authority has to be Federal. In the great flood of 1927, Calvin Coolidge let Herbert Hoover make himself czar of the river system. Hoover, who fostered cartels in industry, declared that prosperity can be organized by "cooperative group effort and planning" — i.e. by coordinating expectations consciously, from the top down. It was too late, however, to keep the power elite of New Orleans, who ran Louisiana, from dynamiting the levee protecting St. Bernard and Plaquemines Parishes, saving the City by flooding the rednecks. These responded by electing Huey Long Governor in 1928, breaking New Orleans' hegemony for good.

Meantime, Hoover and a few rich power-brokers organized the Tri-State Flood Control Commission to coordinate efforts among at least Louisiana, Mississippi, and Arkansas. The upshot was to strengthen Federal authority by giving Federal dollars for levees without requiring any local matching. Coordination was achieved by making local governments plaintive supplicants (like Mayor Nagin and Governor Blanco) at the public trough, brokered by the highly politicized U.S. Army Engineer Corps. Over time this arrangement has entailed less coordination, and more pork-barrel subsidizing of complaisant corruption in local levee districts – the opposite of what San Francisco faced in 1907.

Hoover's czardom also came too late to allocate lands for a bypass or spillway, such as the broad one west of Sacramento that protects the lower Sacramento Valley. Too many oxen would be gored to make good politics. The New Deal did begin the massive program of reservoirs up north, to supplement the levees down south. Well and good, even if you harbor doubts about big dams, but they offered no protection against Katrina's attack from the south, any more than the guns of Singapore, fixed to shoot out to sea, could protect that city from the Japanese overland attack from the north in 1942. The overbuilt levees, legacy of 150 years of the slow vicious spiral of misdirected competition to beggar-thy-neighbor, finally betrayed the city.

What to do now? A strong dose of Georgist tax policy will revive the private sector of any city, and the surrounding rural areas too. As to flood control, we need an integrated system that will sacrifice some lands as spillways to protect others, and a tax system that will compensate the losers (including the landless) from the gains of the winners. Given such integration, engineers since James B. Eads in 1870 have developed workable plans for the whole river system. It would take a catastrophe to shock Americans into such a new mode of thinking – but the catastrophe just occurred, so let's get thinking.

— Dollars and Sense, *March-April, 2006*

What's the Matter with Michigan?

The Rise and Collapse
of an Economic Wonder

In 1995, through an accident of scheduling, two separate meetings were merged at the Levy Institute, Annandale-on-Hudson, NY. It was an odd coupling: one group was of Georgists; the other was of economic advisers to Governor John Engler of Michigan, intent on cutting the property tax. Possibly, we speculated, some hurried planner had confused Michigan's "Single Business Tax" with George's "Single Tax." Still for three days we talked to, or at least past each other.

We warned Michigan about what had happened to California after Prop. 13. In Lansing, however, the die had been cast. Engler's advisors tuned out our words and went home to help him take public schools off the property tax and put them on a sales tax. Michigan's fatal downslide accelerated. Let us trace her path from adolescence and vigor through long dominance down to senility, where famous firms are dying, industrial cities rotting, great universities shedding, public services declining, public schools starving, unemployment soaring, and youth fleeing. Michigan's number of apportioned US Representatives has dropped from 19 in 1960 to 15 in 2000. The great University of Michigan now charges the highest tuition of any public university in the nation. Michigan's "Big Three" auto firms have crashed loudly and publicly.

Mass transit, high wages, and the birth of the auto industry

From 1890-1900 Detroit's population grew, in spite of the depression, by 40%. That was faster than almost all other cities except Cleveland. By 1910 it had boomed another 60%, leading the nation, and by 1920 another 113%. The auto industry did it, but why in Detroit? It helped that Michigan had produced horse-drawn carriages from its hardwood lumber, but so had other places. It was not low wages, for Detroit paid better than most, which of course is why so many people moved there so fast. It was not business-dominated politics, for Michigan was a Bull Moose* state, the first eastern state to adopt the Initiative and Referendum, an early Home-Rule-for-cities state, an early adopter of direct election of US Senators, a high tax state (in an era when most state and local taxes were property taxes). Governor Hazen Pingree's 1897 message to the State Legislature† is a strikingly radical document, even for its times.

Mayor, then Governor, Hazen Pingree (1840-1901), was an early Georgist Progressive. He found city taxes biased for the rich; he changed that, and pushed the single-tax principle. He was a mentor to and model for the Georgist soon-to-be Mayors Tom Johnson and Newton Baker of Cleveland, and Samuel Jones and Brand Whitlock of Toledo. Pingree reformed assessments and raised property taxes in order to provide vital services for working men and their families. Mass transit, then called "traction," was a central issue.

The Progressive and single-tax movements then went hand-in-hand with "traction" in all the growing cities of that,

---

* "Bull Moose" was the nickname for the Progressive Party started by Theodore Roosevelt.

† http://books.google.com/books?id=RfnkAAAAMAAJ.

their Golden Age. Property taxes were to cover fixed costs, so as to keep fares low. Pingree could not sway enough allies to municipalize traction, so instead he subsidized a competing firm, forcing the older one to lower fares and extend service. It is ironic that the traction monopoly that Pingree fought was owned by none other than Tom Johnson.‡ It is one of history's Greek Tragedies: trolleys nursed the auto industry that was later to rise up and slay them.

Pingree plugged for public ownership of city monopolies and for low fares, an attitude that Harold Hoteling and other academics later rationalized as "marginal-cost pricing." Property taxes also paid for police and fire protection, public education, public health, public parks, water, sanitation, welfare — all the public services that make a big city livable, and its small industries viable. Property tax rates of 2.5% were normal; there were no sales, business or income taxes. Detroit's collection of small machine shops, little businesses and services provided a matrix for the famous innovators who were to spawn the auto industry. Jane Jacobs would have venerated it, as she did Tokyo and Birmingham — except that Jacobs dodged the tax side of it.

Land speculation and monopoly were problems, so in 1891 Pingree campaigned for "higher taxes on the vast landed estates of the city," and won. In 1893 a big industry threatened to leave town if its taxes rose. Pingree was losing this battle when he called on his Georgism and raised just the land assessments. This won the support of businesses he had previously alienated (when he had campaigned to soak the rich). Pingree saw that Detroit could raise revenues from industry without driving it away, simply by focusing assessments more on land, less on capital.

The crash of 1893 hit Detroit soon after Pingree became Mayor. The City was riddled with holes held by land speculators.

---

‡   The relationship was complex, but this is part of the process that converted Johnson to become the most prominent Georgist politician — and beloved, successful mayor — of his decade. Think Epiphany on the road to Damascus.

Pingree prevailed on them to let the unemployed plant vegetables there, and "Pingree's Potato Patches" won national renown, inspiring other cities to do likewise. To Pingree, this was a graphic way to demonstrate to his voters, fresh from following the plow, what people can do when given access to land (a goal he had for all industries). He used tax money on welfare for the unemployed, a move that kept labor on hand to man the next industrial boom. His majorities increased with each election.

Pingree also supported academic freedom, a fragile seedling in that era before John Dewey and Alexander Meiklejohn had founded the American Association of University Professors (AAUP) to uphold academic freedom.. He did not quail at retaining economist Edward Bemis, whom Rockefeller's new University of Chicago had just fired for the solecism of supporting the Pullman strikers in 1894. Polite academicians just didn't do things like that then, and seldom do even now, if they want to flourish with the power elite.

In 1897 Pingree became Governor. He centralized the assessment of property taxes, and had the State Board of Tax Commissioners revalue all property. They found so much untaxed land, especially railroad holdings, to put on the rolls that they actually lowered tax rates even as they raised more revenue — a feat that inspired Robert LaFollette across the lake later to emulate in Wisconsin. (Much later, Arthur Laffer failed to duplicate the success in Washington — because Laffer and his boss, Ronald Reagan, never got the point that was so obvious to Pingree: lower bad taxes by raising the good one.)

In the midst of reforms, Pingree died in 1901. He had not worked alone, however, and in 1904 new Governor Fred Warner resumed Pingree's work and in 1908 won his third term. In 1909 Michigan adopted a new constitution with many basic progressive reforms. Detroit grew from 205,000 souls in 1890 to 1,850,000 in 1950, a faster percentage growth rate than any other city, rising to be America's fourth biggest city. This was an extreme case of a national pattern of cities with pro-labor Georgist leadership outgrowing cities run by the opposition. As for urban sprawl, Pingree favored growth without annexation — a principle that later growthmen were to forget, to their sorrow.

Urban sprawl in the 1920's

By 1930 Detroit had 68% more people than in 1920, again leading the nation. 1920s leaders, however, were not like the Progressive Republicans of yore; they were New Era Republicans of what Michigan's Professor Kenneth Boulding was to call "The Cowboy Economy." They twisted Pingree's ideas by growing in area more than they grew in people. Detroit's best-known product, marketed to millions, let builders sprawl over outskirts and suburbs to a degree hitherto unthinkable. Detroit's rich tax base, misspent, helped them do it.

Michigan Business Professor Ernest M. Fisher, normally given to timid understatement, documented the damages in monographs and articles that became minor classics of boom and bust in urban expansion. Most American cities underwent the same process, but Detroit was even more obsessed than most with its new toy, the auto, in which its civic leaders and role models gloried. So, it sprawled beyond the average. Hard-luck Flint became a poster-child victim of sprawl and land speculation, singled out for attention by leading planner Edmund Bacon (1940, "A Diagnosis"). Harold S. Buttenheim, Georgist editor of the then-influential *American City Magazine*, focused on Detroit. Recently, as GM closed down Flint's life-support, Michael Moore republicized Flint as a poster-child. Neither glare of publicity has cured Flint's problems, however. That would require rediscovering the secrets of Hazen Pingree.

Michigan in the Great Depression

Like many cities, Detroit crashed in the "Dirty Thirties," but it did better than most, growing by 3.5%. The world was still discovering the wonders of cars, tractors and trucks. Still, its people knew hard times, and searched for new ideas and leaders. It produced at least three prominent new men from outside the establishment, who led it in the New Deal direction. These were Charles Coughlin, Frank Murphy, and Walter Reuther. Coughlin and Murphy flashed across history's sky and faded. Reuther, working in the grubby trenches and staying home, was to have the more lasting impact.

Fr. Charles Coughlin was pastor of a small church in Royal Oak, a small inner suburb of Detroit. He mastered the new medium of radio, and amassed a huge national following in the early depression years. He saw social salvation in the 1931 Encyclical of Pope Pius XI, *Quadragesimo Anno* (40 Years Later), a rehash/update of Pope Leo XIII's *Rerum Novarum*, 1891. He popularized those messages as never before, partly through good timing: 1891 had been a boom time, while 40 years later, 1931, was a year of bust and social unrest. Both encyclicals bear an uncanny likeness to FDR's New Deal, much of it framed by Irish and other Catholics whom they touched through Coughlin. However, Coughlin's Michigan springboard rocketed him so fast to international prominence that he had little specific role in Michigan.

Frank Murphy, Detroit's Mayor 1930-33, was "a New Dealer before there was a New Deal" (Sidney Fine, biographer, 1984), and helped elect FDR. By all accounts he was of high character and ambition. FDR bundled him off to the Philippines as Governor-General (possibly to exile a potential rival?) Murphy returned to become one of Michigan's few Democratic Governors. During his tenure (1936-38) Walter Reuther's fledgling UAW pioneered the sit-down strike at GM's plant in Flint. Governor Murphy called out the national guard, but refused to authorize violence. Instead he negotiated a settlement that legitimized the UAW, using the new national Wagner Act. It was "The strike heard round the world." UAW membership exploded from 30,000 to 500,000. "Industrial unionism" had arrived to rival and later join the old AFL.

Walter Reuther (1907-1970) was a socialist from a socialist family, and a beaver who came up the hard way, organizing unions in a time of violence when employers controlled the police and the FBI. He survived beatings by strikebreakers, and two assassination attempts, before dying in a mysterious plane crash in 1970. He couldn't get elected even to the Detroit City Council, yet *TIME* magazine included him with the 100 most influential people of the 20th Century. He turned Republican Michigan into a union state, and his union into a major national political force. After 1939 he became a Democrat, increasingly on intimate terms with Party leaders. Even in 2008, Senate Republicans opposed bailing out Detroit auto-makers to avoid helping out Reuther's creation, the UAW.

All this time, with all this excitement, with boom and bust in the land market, Michigan depended mainly on the property tax. From 1932, other states were turning to sales taxes for "property tax relief," but not Michigan, not yet. Doughty Ben Smith of Grand Rapids churned out reams of essays and tables of data demonstrating that states progressed economically in the measure that they used the property tax to finance government. It is tragic he didn't survive to polish and package his works better. They are diamonds in the rough, just waiting for some graduate student to repackage and update them.

Detroit in the arsenal of democracy, 1940-50

After 1941, with "Lend-lease," and especially after Pearl Harbor, FDR naturally turned to Detroit to convert its assembly lines and supply sources to war production. The whole nation revived, but Detroit grew by 14% while most cities grew by much less, and some shrank. This was the age of Rosie the Riveter, but Rosie favored Detroit over most other venues. Walter Reuther the anti-fascist converted to a regular Democrat; Reuther the German-American squelched wildcat strikes against the war effort; Reuther the born Marxist purged communists from his unions, joined the cold war, and rated high in Washington. He was a man for his times. It appeared that Detroit and Michigan were back on the fast track — but not for long.

Famous Governors and meager results, 1950-70

From 1950-60, Detroit shrank by 10%, the first break in its sensational upward trajectory. What could the matter be? "Explainers" could blame the end of the war — but demand for autos and trucks was booming. America was pouring billions into the Interstate Highway System and urban and continental sprawl. The St. Lawrence Seaway was on track to open in 1959. Mass transit was dying. The causes must have been endogenous.

In 1952 Governor G. Mennen "Soapy" Williams was elected. He was the scion of an old Detroit family (Mennen toiletries), handsome, personable, an academic "prodigy," ambitious, cover of *TIME* and presidential timber. Like Murphy, he won as a Democrat in a Republican state. In 1952 the new Governor Williams allied with old labor warrior Reuther, and represented some of his views. He saw a need for more state services. Michigan had no state income tax at that time — only half the states did, and Michigan's neighbors and competitors Indiana, Ohio, and Illinois did not. Taxing "business" may have sounded good to Reuther, the intellectual steeped in Marxist economics.

Williams' 1953 tax was called the Business Activities Tax (BAT). Technically it was an odd duck, a kind of modified VAT that "the business community" preferred to a tax on corporate income, which has a narrower base and therefore requires a higher rate. Michigan overall still grew, as Detroit was hollowing out; but Michigan grew slower than the national average, losing another Congressional seat. It stood still compared with, say, California. As for Williams, he was shuffled off, like Murphy before him, to minor foreign posts. He came home and ended his career as

Chief Justice of the Michigan Supreme Court. His lasting memorial is the long, expensive Mackinac bridge, a 1950s version of a "bridge to nowhere," for it links only to the economically barren Upper Peinsula, which is sterilized by latifundia.

The next famous Governor was George Romney, 1962-68. Boosters proclaimed him a hero because he had rescued American Motors by promoting the Rambler (although it was made in Wisconsin). Romney was a "liberal Republican" (as the term was then understood), loosely allied with Nelson Rockefeller who loaned him economic adviser George Gilder, co-author with Jude Wanniski of early "supply-side" works. Romney viewed Reuther as "the most dangerous man in America" because Reuther had a visionary and idealistic side. It bears noting that Reuther's UAW was integrated racially, and Reuther was a long-time supporter of both Martin Luther King, Jr., and César Chavez. Romney might better have sided with Reuther against primitive Jimmy Hoffa, Reuther's arch-enemy. Romney introduced a personal income tax to help support public schools and provide "property tax relief," a p.r. catchphrase that, alas, caught on. No one seemed to love the property tax, least of all economics professors at the University of Michigan, blind to its earlier role under Pingree and Warner in catalyzing Michigan's amazing growth.

Meanwhile, the property tax itself was degenerating, nationwide, into more of a tax on buildings, less on land, through confusion and corruption in the assessment process. One can trace this openly in professional and scholarly works on assessment. Manuals from the International Association of Assessing Officers (IAAO) grew increasingly muddled.[*] Detroit was assessing land values at next to nil, using assessments dating from the Great Depression, and no one was doing anything about it. Economists weren't even writing about it. Only one Michigan

---

[*] A leading scholarly study from the Harvard University Press (Mabel L. Walker, *Urban Blight and Slums*, 1938) recommended wiping out property taxes altogether.

city, Southfield, made itself an exception with outstanding results, discussed below.

In 1967, a police raid on an unlicensed late-night drinking club in a black neighborhood triggered Detroit's notorious 12th Street riots, which destroyed over 2000 buildings. President Johnson sent in US troops. Police harassment of blacks was consistent with their use of force against the UAW, which Reuther had integrated. Candidate Romney courted blacks more than previous Republicans had, but he was a prominent leader in his Mormon Church. At that time (before 1978) this Church denied blacks its "priesthood" (full membership), and had a long if vague and arguable record of discrimination in its sacred texts, none of which sat well in the new era of civil rights. Governor Romney had been preoccupied during this, his last term, seeking the Republican nomination for US President. The 12th Street Riots damaged both Romney and LBJ so much that both of them dropped out of the race. Romney was condemned for opposing the war, and LBJ for waging it — so, it seems likely that their poor handling of the riots was a more important factor. They never recovered, and neither has Detroit.

In 1967, more quietly, Michigan dropped its "BAT" and replaced it with a regular corporate income tax.*

Southfield booms while Detroit busts

While Detroit hollowed out, its suburb Southfield boomed and grew as fast as Detroit had in its glory days. From

---

* That was a change for the better, but it lasted a mere 7 years, to 1974. It deferred Michigan's worst problems because employers deduct wages from taxable income. In addition they deduct many capital investments. Michigan's Professor Richard A. Musgrave, with co-author Evsey Domar, famously explained in a classic article that deducting capital outlays may lower the effective tax rate to or towards zero. The BAT, by contrast, is on *gross* income, with no deductions.

1950-70 Southfield grew from 19,000 to 69,000 people. It had a Georgist Mayor, James Clarkson, who made a point of raising land assessments and lowering building assessments. How can a mayor do that? Clarkson observed that there is wide latitude in the assessment process — which most assessors use to underassess land. Southfield had been valuing land at 10% or less of market value. In 1960 Clarkson, like Pingree in 1890, campaigned for Mayor to correct that. Meeting resistance, he hired a Georgist assessor, Ted Gwartney, and had him upvalue land and downvalue buildings. Gwartney had honed this skill while working for Dr. Irene Hickman, elected Assessor of Sacramento County, California, who was also a Georgist. Clarkson served four terms before the Michigan powers lured him away with a judgeship. Gwartney left to pursue a distinguished career elsewhere. Southfield immediately leveled off at 76,000 people and has not grown since.

Harvard Law Professor Oliver Oldman, a leading tax authority, scoffed at the evidence at a meeting we both attended. In his view, Southfield was merely taking advantage of Detroit's problems, exploiting white flight. Oldman believed that Southfield was engaging in competitive undertaxation, a "race to the bottom." Such, unfortunately, has been the academic p.c. mindset — but it ain't so. Southfield's tax base actually rose by 20% per year under Clarkson/Gwartney, and it provided good utilities and public services. Even the landowners whose assessments Gwartney raised made out well, because the benefit of the relief of potential buildings from overtaxation was shifted to landowners in the form of higher market values. It was Detroit that was "racing to the bottom."

The "Single Business Tax" (SBT), 1975

In 1975 Michigan adopted its distinctive "Single Business Tax" (SBT), replacing the corporate income tax. This is a variety of VAT, a tax on gross receipts less certain deductions. First, as with any VAT, one deducts purchases from other firms, reasoning they have been taxed already on the value they added. Well and good — that is the virtue of VAT; it prevents "cascading." The awful vice, however, is that the taxed business does *not* deduct labor costs. So, what is touted as a tax on "business" is mainly a tax on the value added by labor, adding damage to deception.

Michigan's SBT has two more especially bad features. One is that unincorporated businesses, mostly small ones, are as subject to the tax as huge corporations. The other is that buying real estate, including land, is deductible as a current expense. This is illogical; land should not even be depreciable, since land does not wear out, and *a fortiori* should not be expensible in the year purchased. Imagine owners A and B selling a parcel of land to each other in alternate years, each buyer expensing it each time! It amounts to a great subsidy for holding land. By 1980 Detroit had dropped another 20% of its people from 1970.

Professors of Economics at the University of Michigan have not warned of or deplored these catastrophes. Rather, they join the power elites pushing the SBT and other variations of VAT. Joel Slemrod and James Hines lead Michigan's Office of Tax Policy Research (OTPR), a venue for dozens of protégés to tout the SBT as a model for all states, and the nation. They supply a toehold inside the USA for the "troika" of international organizations* that are imposing VATs on every other nation. Professor Slemrod, when Editor of the *National Tax Journal,* gave extraordinary fast-track treatment to a manifesto from the OECD pushing for a worldwide VAT. The OTPR has positioned itself at the center of the cobweb of "neo-liberal" research and publishing in public finance in our times. It pushes hard for VAT, in Michigan, in all states, and in the nation. No one at OTPR

---

* The European Central Bank (ECB), European Commission (EC), and the International Monetary Fund (IMF).

has accepted any responsibility for the crash of Michigan, or for Europe's steady decline that has coincided with its heavy reliance on VAT, even as OTPR and its many writers and protégés continue to sing the praises of VAT and urge all to adopt it.

Governor John Engler scuppers the property tax, 1995

In 1995 Governor John Engler decided to heal Michigan by taking its public schools off the property tax, putting them on a state sales tax. The national media commented favorably, crediting California's pioneering Prop. 13. Soon, however, Michigan got sicker. The press of March 11, 2007 reported the following:

☞ Michigan's unemployment rate had been at 7% for four years. Only Mississippi was higher; the national average was 4.6%. Some Michigan counties were at 10% when the Great Recession began. As old industries leave they are not being replaced.

☞ Michigan lost 300,000 jobs, 2000-2008.

☞ Personal income per capita dropped below the national average in 2000 and has stayed below.

☞ 22,500 people aged 18-24 left, 2000-2008.

Note again that first point, "As old industries leave they are not being replaced." What is left behind then but idle land? Once again, Detroit is riddled with holes, and in another of history's ironies people today are growing food in them to subsist — "Pingree's Potato Patches" again, 105 years later.

None of Michigan's postwar efforts at stimulative tax reform, save one, have done the job. That one is Southfield, 1960-1970, which scholars and politicians have studiously ignored. Bellwether Detroit lost 50% of its people between 1950-2000. Flint has lost 40%. Benton Harbor on Lake Michigan is a basket case. Then, to top it off, in 2008 Michigan moved on from mere decline to a Crash heard round the world.

Here is the advice I gave to Gov. Engler's economic advisors at that 1995 Levy Institute conference:

WHAT HAPPENS *when a state radically slashes its property tax? Michiganders are saying they must wait and see, but California can show you 17 years of experience. To read your future, just study our past. Here is what has happened since California passed Proposition 13 in 1978:*

THE OBVIOUS DIRECT RESULTS *have been to cut public services, raise other taxes, and lose credit rating. Our school support fell from #5, nationally, to #40 in 1985 when last seen, and is still falling. County road maintenance is down to where my county (Riverside) is repaving its roads at an annual rate of once every 130 years. Once in 20 years is recommended here, and up north you need higher frequency. You can't just build infrastructure and then stop paying for it. Thanks to urban sprawl, a high fraction of our population now depends on these county roads.*

IN 1978 WE HAD A SURPLUS *in Sacramento. Since then we have raised business taxes, income taxes, sales taxes and gas taxes, but go broke every June. Now our State bond rating is last among the states. One of our richest counties (Orange) has gone bankrupt; Los Angeles is on the brink of it, saving itself by closing emergency rooms and hospitals that serve as a last resort for the uninsured poor.*

THE PRIVATE SECTOR *is doing badly, too. Raising income taxes, business taxes, and sales taxes is no way to stimulate an economy; they are all a drag on work and enterprise. Our per capita income was down from #7 to #12 among the states by 1992, then fell some more. From 1992-94, California was one of three states where median household income fell. Our unemployment rate (2008) is 9%, 50% higher than the national mean of 6%. Our poverty rate is 18%, compared to 14.5% nationally. Not surprisingly, therefore, the only government function that grows now is building and operating prisons. One of our few rebounding industries is cinema, the art of escaping from reality: we excel at that. Another thriving activity is that of auctioning off used machinery for export to the east.*

IN 1993 THERE WAS NET OUTMIGRATION *(including inter-national migration) from this state that has symbolized American growth since time immemorial. It is unheard of. Nearly 2% of the population, 426,000 people, were lost. This is a watershed change: imagine of all states California, America's trend-setter, our El Dorado, The Golden State, our Horn of Plenty, the safety-valve for job-seekers and retirees and entrepreneurs from everywhere, the end of the rainbow, losing population! It's almost enough to make a person click off the tube and think.*

THE FALL *of our per capita income is greater than appears from the purely monetary measure. Real pay has fallen more, because of the drastic rise of shelter prices. In San Francisco, shelter takes 50% of the median income, with many other cities, especially coastal ones, not far behind. The median home price rose 163% during the 1980s, to $258,000 (remember that is just the* median *— the mean is higher). These rises are part of the cost of living for all renters and new buyers, a part not fully incorporated in standard CPI measures.*

SOME CITIES *are in desperate straits. San Bernardino in 1976 was chosen an "All-America City, a City on the Go." It went, all right: today, 40% of its people are on welfare.*

CALIFORNIA *has always been earthquake country, but has al-ways renewed itself, routinely. It was different after the Northridge quake in the San Fernando Valley, January, 1994. This is the upper-middle class neighborhood of Los Angeles, but now large pockets of ruined buildings remain, unreconstructed, inhabited only by vagrants and criminals: an instant Bronx West. These blighted sections, ominous portents, spread more blight around them.*

IT SHOULD GIVE ONE PAUSE. *It is, however, if you think about it, the expectable result of what the voters did. They turned property from a functional concept into a sacred one. Instead of a commission to be enterprising, hire people, produce goods, and pay taxes, real property became a welfare entitlement. California's voters (whether they real-ized it or not) rejected the concept of a tax on inert wealth in favor of taxing liquidity and cash flow. The predictable result is to inhibit economic activity, and encourage holding wealth inert and stagnant.*

WE HAD A CONSTRUCTION BOOM in the 1980s, but it was not healthy. It was marked by extreme sprawl, and extreme instability. Downtown LA was to become a great new financial capital, but now has nearly the highest office vacancy rate in the US, with of course a high rate of builder bankruptcies. Speculative builders were led on to over-build, in part, by anticipated higher land rents and prices. This Lorelei effect was magnified by national income-tax provisions luring on specu-lative builders, but we have to ask why California fell harder than other states, even with the object-lessons of the oil states in clear view.

DAVID SHULMAN tersely summarized the distributive effects of Prop. 13 as he left us for Salomon Brothers in Manhattan: "it breached the social compact." Alienation is the result, and the Rodney King riots, arson and looting are the results of alienation. True, the Watts riots preceded Prop. 13, but they were part of a national epidemic. By 1967 there were riots with arson and looting in 70 or more American cities. The Rodney King riots were endemic to California, and spread over a much wider area of Los Angeles than the Watts riots did. The looters and arsonists were not all black, and the targets were not all white, but mainly Korean-Americans who just happened to be there minding their stores.

CONVENTIONAL WISDOM blames our bust on the end of the Cold War. Surely that is a factor, but as a causal explanation it is too pat, too easy and a-historical. Compare today with 1945. Los Angeles's economy depended much more on The Hot War, 1940-1945, than it ever did on The Cold War. Los Angeles's wartime boom had swelled its population as no other great city, 1940-45. After 1945 the US pulled the plug on defense spending far more abruptly than today. Jane Jacobs, in The Economy of Cities, *tells us what happened to military spending in Los Angeles after 1945. It lost 3/4 of its aircraft workers, and 80% of its shipbuilders. It lost its military and naval overseas supply and replacement businesses. Troops stopped funneling through. It got worse: petroleum and cinema and citrus, its traditional exports, all declined.*

PUNDITS FORECASTED A REGIONAL COLLAPSE. *Yet Los Angeles never collapsed, nor missed a beat. The wartime immigrants stayed put here. They formed creative, innovative small businesses in large numbers, giving LA its deserved reputation for having the most dynamic, flexible, adaptable industrial base in the nation. Besides exporting goods, LA also became more self-contained, providing itself with more of the goods it previously imported. How could this be?*

ONE OF EVERY EIGHT *new businesses started in the US were in LA, 1945-50. These were small, creative and flexible, too varied to classify. No Linnaeus could sort them in conventional categories: the new Angelenos simply stayed here and started producing everything for themselves, some things previously imported, and others never seen before. Eastern firms established branch plants here. Top eastern students came to California's great university system, and stayed behind to make careers and jobs here. There was a kind of regional "El Dorado Effect," as demand and supply grew together, and growing local demand allowed for economies of scale serving local markets. Food and shelter were cheap and abundant. Land for business was accessible, providing a basis for the whole self-contained phenomenon. A "continental tilt" developed in both interest rates and wage rates, drawing in eastern capital and labor.*

WHY IS THAT NOT HAPPENING TODAY, 1995? *Because Proposition 13 makes it possible to hold land at negligible tax cost. In 1945 land was taxed at 3% every year, building a fire under holdouts to turn their land to use. Today that same tax cost is well below 1%. Using Gwartney's Rule of Thumb [for 1995 California assessments], it is about 1/8 of 1%: a rate of 1% applied to 1/8 of the true value.*

LANDOWNERS *are only taxed now if they use their land to hire people and produce something useful. Then they meet the drag of our high business and employment and sales taxes, necessitated by the fall of property taxes. A handful of oligopolistic landowners control most of the market; small businesses are squeezed out. This helps us segue from being at the cutting edge of industrial progress to a third-world* economy — *from the New Hampshire model to the Alabama model* — *with no relief in sight.*

WHAT WAS DIFFERENT THEN? *One obvious difference was the high property tax dependence in 1945, and the lower burdens of sales tax, business tax, and income tax. We not only had high property tax rates, they were more focused on land then than now. In 1917, California tax valuers focused on land value so much that it constituted 72% of the assessment roll for property taxation — a much higher fraction than today. This became the California tradition.*

IN 1934 *the "EPIC" campaign of Upton Sinclair* included a strong Georgist element — he proposed to set up new factories on idle land. Meantime, Jackson Ralston was pushing a purer land tax initiative, 1934-38. Ralston lost, but the mere existence of such political action in California, when the movement was torpid elsewhere, tells us a lot. It reveals a large matrix of supportive voters and workers to whom politicians (including tax assessors) would naturally respond by focusing on land assessments.*

CALIFORNIA DISPLAYED AMAZING GROWTH *up to 1978, and the resilience to shrug off the loss of war industries after 1945 and still grow "explosively" (as Jane Jacobs put it). After 1978 we had a string of reverses. The timing, a* priori *causative analysis, and numerous direct observations support an hypothesis that the reverses were aggravated by Prop. 13. Michigan, be warned of our lot, and learn about taxes from us:* **THIS COULD HAPPEN TO YOU.**

— *Groundswell*, November 2008

---

* EPIC, End Poverty In California, was the slogan for Sinclair's 1934 campaign for Governor of California.

Economics in Support of Environmentalism

"**E**conomics in support of environmentalism" — is that an oxymoron? There are economists who put down environmentalists as unwelcome intruders in social policy; there are environmentalists who file economists under "The Great Satan..." Some economists deserve it. I will show how these differences arise, and how they may be composed.

Worthy goals often conflict with each other

Growing barley is a worthy goal (especially if you enjoy a little beer). So is growing corn. It would be great to raise as much of each as anyone wants, but the Earth has its limits. A choice and a decision are required. People invented (or stumbled into) the discipline of economics to help with such hard choices, and to console ourselves that we are doing the right thing. The hardest choices are those regarding land use, because there is just so much. We can build more houses, cars, and boats, write more music and drama, spawn and educate more people, but we cannot make another Hudson Valley.

Barley grows on cheap land, and the demand is limited, so the best barley land is used for growing corn. Economics reconciles the competing demands and rationalizes the outcome. It defines the "highest and best use" of land as that yielding the highest net gain, the excess of revenues over costs. Economists include non-cash "service flows" among "revenues," (although they bear watching: sometimes they forget). Thus, economics shows how the market sorts and arranges land uses, giving us a corn belt, a wheat belt, and a cotton belt. Economists pride themselves on this achievement.

By the same logic, irrigated crops take land from dry-farmed crops; orchards take land from irrigated row crops; housing takes land from orchards and groves; commerce takes land from housing.

Sometimes the rich take land from the poor, provoking sympathy, strong rhetoric, and occasionally effective rearguard resistance to such changes. Actually, a well-oiled market is often quite democratic. People of moderate income, by crowding, can outcompete those of high income for the same land, as when a Sears or Walmart takes the best commercial sites from a Nordstroms or Macys; or when an old estate is subdivided into five lots per acre. This, too, provokes negative rhetoric, but developers know how to make hay out of this: they become populists and accuse preservationists and environmentalists of snobbery and elitism. We need an answer for that one, if environmentalists are going to command enough popular support to win, and hold the gains. Of this, more later.

Other worthy goals that conflict are open space and water conservation. A major problem in an arid land is that much wide open space guzzles up water. Conserving open space and conserving water conflict directly. Green grass uses more water per acre than almost any farm crop except rice (and rice returns part of it downstream). In cities most water is used not for swimming pools or toilets or washing machines, but for sprinkling lawns. Cemeteries, golf courses, horse-pastures, parks, freeway banks, and the spacious tax-exempt grounds of institutions are the greatest water junkies, outside of farming itself, which takes much more, all told, than cities do.

Something has to give. Thus far it has been wetlands that gave. Once, perhaps, we had too much wetland, but that was long ago. We cannot accommodate all those uses, and save wetlands too, just by having restaurants stop serving water, or putting bricks in toilet tanks. Those are just token or "Goo-goo" measures for parlor reformers; they distract us from real problems, and substitute for real solutions. What is the highest and best use of water? It may well be wetlands, not golf courses. But we need a rule to gauge "highest and best use." Is it the market?

Some of the losers in the market game are not willing to grin and bear it. Instead, they write new rules; they want to play a different game. Soilsmen did this long since. They like to classify land and rank it by its potentiality for growing crops. Farming is, to them, the ultimate value, so it is the highest and best use: cities may have what's left over. It is perhaps poetic justice that habitat-savers are now doing the same thing to farmers. They conceive highest use as that which saves endangered species: soils and farming may be damned, right along with housing, commerce, transportation, industry, storage, water supply, waste disposal, fire control, education, religion, mining, government, national defense, recreation, and whatever else needs land. Land is needed for all human activities, and survival itself — so that list is a long one. Each constituent of the other uses becomes an enemy.

Thus, to restore citriculture and habitat in what is now Los Angeles, we would move the city folks to hazard-prone floodplains, steep slopes subject to fire and erosion, quake-prone fault lines and liquefiable soils, etc. We would also move them away from the center, imposing longer commutes, greater auto-dependency, longer utility lines, longer hauls to dispose of solid wastes, more air to protect, more aquifer surface to protect, more land to protect from flooding, etc.

Sometimes preservationism, like any good cause given power, runs completely amok and makes itself ridiculous. For example, in Downey, California, the Los Angeles Conservancy and the National Register of Historic Places are fighting hard to save — I am not making this up — a McDonald's drive-in, complete with neon sign!

They are serious! Governor Wilson weighed in with this outburst of California pride: "The modern history of McDonald's will be as important to the cultural history of our nation as the invention of Coca Cola." (That comparison seems apt enough.) "Preserve for posterity the home of McDonald's golden arches!"

In Victoria, B.C., the University of Victoria bars people from 2-3 acres of its tax-free campus to preserve habitat for its nesting skylarks, an endangered species. Never mind that they are an import from England, like starlings: now they are being "preserved" to keep things natural. Likewise, a certain residence on a steep slope in the arid Malibu Hills contains an artificial pond, filled with pumped water, but adorned with reeds "to keep it natural."

Both soilsmen and habitat-persons will become isolated and ineffective unless they forswear extremism, and modify their new rules to accommodate other worthy goals with other constituencies. Until then, they will appear to others to be single-valued ideologues, fundamentalists with siege mentalities. To succeed they — we — must learn to lead larger alliances by offering more complete philosophies and guidelines for policy.

The dereliction of economists

There is another kind of fundamentalist, the private property kind. The economics profession (my tribe) has, in recent years, largely abdicated its proper role as an arbitrator and gone over to the side of private-property extremism. This is the essential meaning of "Neoclassical Economics," which is the idiom of most discourse in the field today.

How did economics get so twisted? Don't blame Adam Smith, or David Ricardo, or John Stuart Mill, or John E. Cairnes, or Knut Wicksell, or Philip Wicksteed, sterling 19th Century writers. Rather, blame John Bates Clark, Karl Marx, Richard T. Ely, Alvin Johnson, Frank Fetter, Frank Knight, George Stigler, and a host of lesser figures who gradually warped economics into its present form. How did they do it?

Defining away land

They wiped out land, resources, nature, and the environment as a separate class for analysis. In official Neoclassical doctrine, the world is an infinite reservoir of raw land and resources. Raw land has no value until man does two things:

1. Man subjects land to private tenure. The very act of privatizing land gives it value it lacked before. Land without an owner has no value — take that, Aldo Leopold! You will find this in J.B. Clark, 1886, *The Philosophy of Wealth*. Clark points out that wealth is created "from the mere appropriation of limited natural gifts...." The atmosphere as a whole, showers or breezes, "minister transiently to whomsoever they will, and, in the long run, with impartiality." Therefore they are not wealth. Those who appropriate them create wealth by so doing. The essential attribute of wealth is "appropriability," to create which "the rights of property must be recognized and enforced.... Whoever makes, interprets, or enforces law produces wealth." It follows that those who pollute the common air, or anything held in common, are not damaging anything of value, since it belongs to no one.

Clark writes of "the essential wealth-constituting attribute of appropriability." He goes on in that vein: those who seize land and exclude others thereby produce its value. Clark founded Neoclassical economics, and is emulated closely by the "New Resource Economists" of today.

2. Man improves the raw land, pumping value into it. After that it is just like any man-made capital. Raw land has no value: God contributed nothing. Consistently with this worldview, merely eyeing the General Sherman redwood tree adds nothing to GNP, but cutting it down would add a lot. Eyeing it would only raise GNP if you had to pay for it, or had to drive a long way to get there, and bought a kewpie doll while you were there. Likewise, commuting 80 miles a day raises GNP, while finding a homesite near work lowers it.

Private property: from means to end

In a proper view of things, I submit, private property is a means to an end. It is not an end in itself; it needs a functional rationale. The end is to get land put to the best use. All the private land in the world was originally granted by some sovereign public person or body, mainly for that purpose, not as a welfare entitlement. Landowners and their lawyers have slyly, over time, turned the means into an end, a fetish they endow with "sanctity." This is a term they borrowed from absolutist medieval theology. "Sanctity" means the quality or state of being holy or sacred, hence inviolable. It means property may not be challenged, or even questioned. It has become an end in itself, its own voucher. You're not supposed to think about it.

The Neoclassical economists' view of their proper role is rather like that in The Realtor's Oath, which includes a vow "To protect the individual right of real estate ownership." The word "individual" is construed broadly to include corporations, estates, trusts, anonymous offshore funds, schools, government agencies, institutions, partnerships, cooperatives, the Duke of Westminster, the Sultan of Brunei, the Medellin Cartel, congregations, Archbishops, families (including criminal families) and so on, but "individual" sounds more all-American and subsumes them all. This is a potent chant that stirs people to extremes of self-righteousness and siege mentality when challenged.

The resemblance between Neoclassical economics and the Realtor's Oath is easier to understand when you learn that Professor Richard T. Ely, founder of the modern discipline of Land Economics, was heavily subsidized by the National Association of Real Estate Boards, the utilities, the major landowning railroads, and others of like mind and property interests.

When it comes to violating property rights, air pollution today is perhaps the greatest invader and confiscator of property. Where do economists stand? Once a few of them tried to say, following A.C. Pigou, "let the polluter pay," and in parts of Europe they still do. In our modern backward thinking here at home, however, it's not the polluter who is invading the property of others, nor the human rights of those not owning property. Rather, when you tell them to stop, the government is invading *their* rights. The wage-earning taxpayers must pay them to stop, else you are violating both the 14th Amendment and the "Coase Theorem," a rationalization for polluting now dearly beloved by Neoclassical economists.

Leapfrogging, floating value and compensation

The environmental damage from those attitudes might not be so bad were it not for leapfrogging, urban disintegration, and floating value. Leapfrogging is when developers jump over the next eligible lands for urban expansion, and build farther out, here and there. This has been a problem in expanding economies ever since cities emerged from within their ancient walls and stockades, but in our times and our country it has gone to unprecedented extremes, with subsidized superhighways and universal auto ownership and truck shipping.

Alfred Gobar, savvy real estate consultant from Placentia, has recorded the amount of land actually used by city and suburban dwellers for all purposes. From this, he calculates that the entire US population could live in the state of Missouri (68,965 square miles). That would be at a density of 3,625 people per square mile, fewer than 6 per acre. That is 7,683 square feet per person. On a football gridiron, this is the area from the goal to the 16-yard line.

He is not being stingy with land, at 3,625 persons per square mile. The population density of Washington, DC, is 10,000 per square mile, with a 10-story height limit, with vast areas in parks, wide baroque avenues and vistas, several campuses, and public buildings and grounds. This is also the density of Whitefish Bay, Wisconsin, a well-preserved upper-income residential suburb of Milwaukee, with generous beaches and parks, tree-lined streets, detached dwellings, retailing, and a little industry. San Francisco, renowned for its liveability, has 15,000 per square mile. More than half the land is in nonresidential uses: vast parks, golf courses, huge military/naval bases, water surface, industry, a huge regional CBD, etc., so the actual residential density is over 30,000 per square mile.

On Manhattan's upper East Side they pile up at over 100,000 per square mile. They do not crowd like this out of desperation, either. You may think of rats in cages, but some of the world's wealthiest people pay more than we could dream about to live that way. They'll pay over a million dollars for less than a little patch of ground: all they get is a stratum of space about 12 feet high on the umpteenth floor over a little patch of ground they share with many others. They could afford to live anywhere: they choose Manhattan. They actually like it there!

Take 10,000 per square mile as a reference figure, because it is easy to calculate with, and because it works in practice, as noted. You may observe and experience it. At that density, 250 million Americans would require 25,000 square miles, the land in a circle with radius of 89 miles, no more. That gives a notion of how little land is actually demanded for full urban use. It is 9.4% as big as Texas, 4.2% as big as Alaska, and 0.7% of the area of the United States.

And yet, the urban price influence of Los Angeles extends over 89 miles east-southeast clear to Temecula and Murrieta and beyond, at which point, however, it meets demand pushing north from San Diego. Urban valuation fever thus affects much more land than can ever actually be developed for urban use. Regardless, most owners come to imagine they might cash in at a high price, with high zoning, at their own convenience, with public services supplied by "the public, " meaning other taxpayers. This is the meaning of "floating value."

If their land is downzoned for farming, open space, or habitat, they regard it as a "taking," and demand compensation, pleading the 14th Amendment. Once we buy into the Sanctity of private property, we owe them. If we think of the public's buying large quantities of it to preserve habitat or open space, the price is already high above its aggregate value, and the new demand will push the price higher yet.

Here is a case showing how this works. The Los Angeles Metropolitan Transit Authority needed the old Union Station, northeast of downtown in a run-down neighborhood, as the center-piece of its new, integrated mass transit system. With the decline of interurban passenger rail traffic, the old station was unused. The own-ers, mainly Southern Pacific, asked more than MTA offered, so MTA invoked its power of eminent domain and condemned the land. The case went to judgment, and in 1984 the court awarded SP an amount about twice the going price for land in the area. The court's reason was that the coming of mass transit would raise values around the new central station, and SP should be paid as much as neighboring landowners would be able to get after the station was built.

Thus, land originally granted to SP to help subsidize mass transit was used instead to obstruct and penalize mass transit. Private property had become an end in itself, Holy and Sacred, a welfare en-titlement, rather than a means to an end. MTA (the taxpayers) had to pay a price for land based on the unearned increment that its own construction and operation was expected to create in the future.

Later, MTA was to stint on subway construction, resulting in subsidence on Hollywood Boulevard, but there was no stinting on paying off SP for doing nothing: the award came to $84.7 mil-lion. This is how the 14th Amendment works in practice, making private property an end, sanctified for its own sake, rather than a means to a higher end. It makes landowners the spoiled children of the national family, inflating the cost of every program that entails acquiring land. It means there is no chance that the public, whether through government or the Nature Conservancy, can preserve more than token areas of habitat by buying it: it would bankrupt us.

Siege mentalities

The result of these trends is to put conservationists-environ-mentalists-ecologists under siege. Here is a sharp, clear statement of it from Vivian Null, San Bernardino Audubon Society: "Once humans lived in small groups surrounded by expanses of wilderness. Today, human civilization has pushed our natural world into ever smaller, fragmented pockets of deteriorating habitat. As a result, we are living in an age of mass extinction."

I sympathize with the view expressed, and understand what outrages provoked it. When it comes to solutions, however, we have a problem. Being under siege fosters a siege mentality. To the layman, self-styled "hard" Scientists can seem more hardheaded and hardball than scientific. They can seem single-valued, self-righteous and — dare I say it? — even a bit arrogant.

At the same time landowners also feel under siege. You may observe how developers rage about having their land set aside for the likes of Stephens Kangaroo Rats, Three-toed Lizards, and California Gnatcatchers. The ideology of Science and the ideology of Private Property have become clashing absolutes. What can we do? It helps to read some history of the successful Conservation Movement of the Progressive Era.

Defining "Conservation"

Gifford Pinchot was a great leader of the Conservation Movement. He defined his central term, conservation, as "The greatest good for the greatest number for the longest time."

Caviling theorists sometimes pick at that famous phrase, since you cannot maximize three things at the same time, but that is unfair, since he was not being technical. He was making a speech, and obviously what he meant was that those three elements should all be considered, and none was to be slighted.

Notice especially the middle clause, for the greatest number. Conservation was not just for landowners, or any other elite. Conservation was part of the Progressive Movement, which had sprung from the Populist Movement. Social equity was at its core. Here is some more of Pinchot's speech (to the 1st National Conservation Congress, 1909):

... the third principle of conservation... is this: the natural resources must be developed and preserved for the benefit of the many and not merely for the profit of a few. ... public action for public benefit has ... a much larger part to play than was the case ... before certain constitutional arrangements ... had given so tremendously strong a position to vested rights and property in general. ... by reason of the 14th Amendment to The Constitution, property rights in the U.S. occupy a stronger position than in any other country in the civilized world. It becomes then a matter of multiplied importance, when property rights once granted are so strongly entrenched, that they shall be granted only under such conditions as that the people shall get their fair share of the benefit which comes from the development of the country which belongs to us all. The time to do that is now.

You modern habitat-savers, your foes score points against you by calling you "elitists." Sure enough, you do appear a bit above, and therefore outside the mainstream, especially when you talk down to people from the eminence of "Science." Pinchot saw that brick coming and dodged it before it was even thrown. He teamed up with the populists; he spoke as a man for the people, even if not quite of them. Can you say the same? Is there a place in your plans, and your hearts, for Joe Sixpack?

When the Southern California Association of Governments (SCAG) surveyed public opinion on policy issues, preserving habitat and endangered species were not even among the top 17 priorities listed by citizens. Neither were private property rights. Their top three concerns are crime, education, and jobs. Politicians have preempted the crime issue, but no one is doing a thing this year for education and jobs. Take a leaf from the successful Gifford Pinchot: team up with some populists. Move into the vacuum left behind the gale of anti-crime oratory. No one is serving the constituency for education and jobs. Other populist issues high on the SCAG list are homelessness, affordable housing, job training, and child care.

Finding common ground

On what basis shall habitat-savers identify with median Americans? We share a problem: we are all victims of private property rights carried to extremes. Abraham Lincoln, the original Radical Republican, once spoke to the effect that whenever landless people cannot find work and shelter, then the rights of private property have been carried too far and must be curbed.

Here are some ideas. First, environmentalists might rethink what we mean by "open space." To Gifford Pinchot, "open" meant the space had public access. Today it often means the reverse: golf courses, duck clubs, sacred Indian lands, private beaches, cemeteries, farmlands, vacant speculative holdings, unpoliced parks taken over by gangs, protected and posted habitat, water from which swimmers are excluded for power boats, rights-of-way closed to hikers, university experimental plots, and so on. In this sense, there is more open land in downtown Manhattan than in many of our rural and sylvan areas. Many a water reservoir is open to beavers, ducks and geese, who routinely powder their noses there, but not to humans who seldom do, and can be trained not to.

To get more support for habitat, find ways to open it to people, putting more funds and effort into behavioral controls if necessary. In Pinchot's day, people spoke unblushingly of "character training," and practiced it. Pinchot himself said, "the training of our people in citizenship is as germane to [conservation] as the productiveness of the earth." Wilderness clubs preached and taught responsible behavior in the wilds. The Boy Scouts taught it, churches taught it, schools taught it, forest rangers taught it, camp managers taught it, community leaders taught it: you heard it all around, and it did help shape your character. It was a great community effort, enlisting broad support and conviction. Then, in that less mobile, less commercialized, more communitarian age, social control over public behavior came naturally. We came to take it for granted, until it silently slipped away. Today it may take more conscious effort, but it was done then, it can be done now.

Second, go with the flow for economy in government. For most of our lives now, we have looked to big government to resolve disputes by buying out both parties. We would have government pay top dollar for land, if needed, and then hire scientists to manage it for habitat. Thus, both sides dream of cutting into line at the government trough: but the trough is empty, and the taxpaying public is in a foul mood. Rather, let's look for ways to cut spending by curbing subsidies to urban sprawl.

Pinchot on "Development"

Gifford Pinchot, the father of Conservation, was not against developing land. In his own words:

> *The first principle of conservation is development, the use of the natural resources now existing ... for the benefit of the people who live here now. There may be just as much waste in neglecting the development and use of certain natural resources as there is in their destruction by waste.... Conservation, then, stands emphatically for the use of substitutes for all the exhaustible natural resources, ...* [water power and water transportation are his examples]. *The development of our natural resources and the fullest use of them for the present generation is the first duty of this generation.*

In the second place conservation stands for the prevention of waste. So Pinchot was against waste, so what? Who isn't? This could be just a banality, but he gives it a new turn. To him, waste means failing to use renewable resources. Today, urban land is the best example.

Urban land is a renewable resource? Economists (who are not all bad) classify urban land as a "flow resource." They liken it to flowing water because its services perish with time, whether used or not, as we are trapped in the one-way flow of time. Likewise, urban land is not depleted by use. It is an even better example of a "flow resource" than flowing water, because, as we are so conscious today, "unharnessed" flowing water may have other downstream uses. Even in wasting out through the Golden Gate, it may repel salinity. The unreaped harvests of idle land, however, flow down the river and out the gates of time, to sink into the past beyond recall, like lost loves dimming in memory, and golden moments we let pass.

What is the "service" of urban land, that we should be mindful of it? For one thing, using central urban land conserves all the hydrocarbons and other resources otherwise needed to traverse it. Compact urban settlement is a direct substitute for oil, with all that implies — and it implies a great deal, which I will leave you to fill in.

Second, using good central land saves all the costs of settling on other land — including the cost of taking more of the shrinking habitat from endangered species. Therefore, habitat-savers should emulate Pinchot and favor development in the right places, the better to oppose it in the wrong places. This is the great lost secret of conservation our times have forgotten. You cannot beat development by opposing it everywhere it pops up. People need land for all kinds of legitimate things, and they will have it. To stop urban sprawl, you must support compact, efficient urban development, including healthy, timely renewal of older cities, inner suburbs, and neighborhoods.

We have met the enemy, and it is US (Urban Sprawl). Let's analyze this beast.

a. Development is not identical with Sprawl. Urban sprawl, which creates a psychological effect of great crowding, is not the product of development as such, but of leapfrogging. Leapfrogging means development in the wrong places. Infilling, on the other hand, is anti-sprawl. It is the cure for sprawl.

b. Sprawl is not a quest for open space. A common belief is that the search of open space is the main force behind sprawl. You may test that by observing high density, cookie-cutter subdivisions scattered throughout the land. Within each such development, you are living at downtown densities. It is when you get onto the freeway to commute, or shop, or take the kids to school or the dentist, or worship, that you experience open space. You experience it as a negative resource, an obstacle between where you are and where you want to go.

c. Sprawl is not the product of free choice. A favorite fallacy is that sprawl results from free individual choice. In fact, sprawl results mainly from subsidies to sprawl, enforced through taxation and/or utility rate regulation. Thus it is imposed, not freely chosen. The classic case, which exemplifies the whole genus, is postal service. It costs you 46¢ to send a letter across the street downtown, or from rural Idaho to rural Florida. The generic name for such subsidies to sprawl is "postage-stamp pricing" (a species of spatial cross-subsidy), which gives you the idea.

In British Columbia, people move around a good deal by car-ferry, because of the terrain. The Provincial Government runs the system. There are many lovely little islands in the Straits of Georgia, between Vancouver Island and the mainland, favored by the wealthy, the exclusive and reclusive. Being more sybaritic than Henry D. Thoreau, and politically puissant, they have demanded and received car-ferry service. This service costs about $10 for every $1 in revenue. The resulting deficit is covered by raising rates on the main plebeian line, Victoria-Vancouver. Naturally, these cheap ferries attract new visitors to the islands, and new demand for land there.

d. Looking for Mr. Goodbar. Here is how we get urban sprawl with leapfrogging. Remember the last time you moved and went househunting? You saw some mouthwatering homes, but they were not for sale. You had to find motivated sellers, and pick from what they offered. It's the same with builders. They scour the exurbs seeking motivated sellers. Ideally the most motivated sellers would line up by distance from the existing city, but the market is not ideal. Each seller is moved by his personal circumstances, not the geographical location.

Potential builders are little concerned with the social costs they might impose, so long as others are to bear them. Thus, they sometimes settle for and build on steep lands with flammable brush and erosion problems, on flood plains, on soils subject to liquefaction in quakes, in canyons and arroyos, on lands with limited access for emergency equipment. They even build on lands without water supply, even in arid southern California, then demand water and get it, secure in the knowledge that Sacramento rejected a recent move to ban development in areas with no assured water supply.

e. The public pays twice. Let's go back to those Channel Islands in British Columbia, with subsidized car-ferries. Naturally, as I said, these cheap ferries attract new visitors to the islands, and new demand for land there. Developers and hopeful subdividers bid up land prices. This is not what the old settlers had in mind: their environment is threatened, including the habitat of endangered species. They appeal to the Crown, which subsidizes their ferries, to help them preserve land for habitat.

They want the government to buy some of it, paying the high prices created by the ferry subsidy, to keep it from use by people who might use the ferries. Thus the government would pay twice: to subsidize the ferries, and then to retire the land at the high prices made possible by the ferries. Failing that, they want the Crown to downzone most of it. The landowners are not charged when the ferries raise their asking prices, but demand compensation when downzoned.

Here, in microcosm, is the American problem with sprawl and habitat. Multiply that ferry subsidy a thousand times, and you have the Great American System of Public Works and Services for Private Gain. First the public pays to bring urban demand to remote lands; now the landowners, the spoiled children of the national family, demand to be paid again for downzoning or selling that same land to preserve habitat. They demand payment not to cash in on the opportunities we just gave them free.

Thus far, it is true, the courts have let us downzone without compensating. However, now a storm has gathered. Proposition

300, on the ballot in Arizona, demands compensation for down-zoning — it is aimed at the Clean Water Act and the Endangered Species Act. There is a movement in Congress to compensate for any Federal regulation that devalues land by more than 50%. It is led by Congressman Billy Tauzin, a Democrat from Louisiana. You can imagine what a more conservative Congress might do. Speculative landowners may soon get everything they demand, leaving heavy debts to which their light tax payments now contribute very little.

Proactive solutions

How do we dig out from this one? I'll repeat: go with the flow of cutting public spending by cutting down subsidies to urban sprawl. They are a major source of the problem. We'll never win the environmental fight until those subsidies are withdrawn.

A second proactive solution is to motivate and help the owners of good land to sell or develop it. To help them, make infilling a positive goal. If you put impost fees on new buildings, do so only in outlying areas that require new public services, not on new buildings that help renew places like South Central L.A. If you ration sewer hookups, save them for central land with street improvements already in place.

Those are the carrots. A good stick is also needed. We have seen how leapfrogging results from the scattered locations of motivated sellers. We can motivate sellers near-in, and in compact increments as we expand spatially, by raising land taxes there.

I could wax rhapsodic about the results to expect from such taxation, but have done so elsewhere and will leave it with a word: visit Sydney, Adelaide, Brisbane, Copenhagen, or Johannesburg, which have made use of this principle to excellent effect.

Dig Deep

These are basic issues, and call for bold actions. Do not waste your time on wimpish meliorism, or "Goo-goo" thinking. Rather, let us study how to emulate the model of Butchart Gardens, near

Victoria, B.C. Butchart doesn't sound like a name for a gardener, and sure enough, Mr. Butchart was a hardrock miner who dug up rocks and left a great ugly gash in the earth. Ah, but Mrs. Butchart, she wanted space for a garden, so she made one there. She rediscovered the truth that land is not just the matter that occupies space, it is space, always renewable and reclaimable. Now Butchart Gardens is one of the world's great beauty spots, drawing visitors from everywhere — in the summertime you hear every language there. Our decayed central cities, too, may bloom again like Mrs. Butchart's garden. Let us make it our model.

Adapted from a paper presented at Community Stewardship of Environmental Resources, a program sponsored by The Community Regional and Environmental Studies Program (CRES), Bard College, October 1994

The Unplumbed Revenue Potential of Land

"You see, but you do not observe." — *Holmes*

I. Pervasive underestimation of land value in current data

The revenue potential of land is greater than anyone thinks. It shouldn't need to be said (yet somehow does) that the purpose of raising more land revenues is not to fatten vexatious bureaucrats, but to replace vexatious taxes, to provide needed public infrastructure and services (including a reasonable national defense), to pay off public debts, and to fund social dividends (including existing social dividends like Social Security). Our task is to identify and uncloset elements of enhanced revenue potential by using truer and more comprehensive measures of rent and land values.

There are at least fifteen elements of land's taxable capacity that previous researchers have either trivialized, or overlooked entirely. First, we will consider corrections for the downward bias in standard data. Then we will expand the concepts of land and its rent, to encompass their true breadth. Finally we'll show how exempting production, trade and capital uncaps potential tax revenues.

Standard data sources neglect and understate real estate rents and values. These standard sources are both local — assessed valuations used for property taxation, and national — as reported by various national agencies, most of whom use IRS data on reported rents.

The local problem: how assessments get so wrong

I will only enumerate, with little elaboration, the many reasons assessed values usually fall short of the market. Scanning the bullets below, however, gives a clue as to how landowner pressure has subverted the property tax over the years.

☞ Conventional use of fractional assessments in many states (the property tax rate is applied not to the full valuation but to a percentage thereof, which has the effect of masking increasingly fictitious valuations).

☞ Lag of assessments behind the rise of land values, and behind the fall of building values with depreciation and obsolescence. Increasingly, this extra-legal process has been institutionalized, as in California's Prop. 13. The bias is against intensive uses at every margin between lower and higher uses.

☞ Use of capitalized income method for assessing business properties (other than apartments, which are often overassessed).

☞ Conventional preference given to acreage, regardless of location, regardless of industrial use. (Allis-Chalmers's large plant in the center of West Allis, Wisconsin, for example, was assessed several times lower per square foot than the adjacent parcels.)

☞ Classification of land for taxation, with preferential low assessment for lower uses (rarely are assessments above the market for any use, except apartments and rentals for the poor). In California, some favored use-classes are farming, timber, and golf. Alabama has another set of low-tax classes, favoring land in forests and hunting grounds, catering to the Heston vote in league with absentee corporate owners (and, for no visible theological reason, organized fundamentalists). Lands in classified uses are assessed by capitalizing their visible money income from the official use only, thus exempting from the tax base all values from rustic manorial, recreational, and bloodsport uses, and all speculative values based on higher future uses. In vast rural and sylvan areas these other influences are the main source of market value.

☞ Assessments capped by zoning, even when the market does not believe the zoning will endure, or be enforced.

☞ Regressive assessments, swayed by case law which reflects differential ability to finance lawsuits and appeals.

☞ Discounts for large lots or other holdings that would sell for a price based on their potential for being subdivided.

☞ Failure to publicize assessed values. In some states the values are not even open to public inspection.

☞ Reluctance to recognize the premium for plottage potential (the gain in value per square foot when small lots are combined, say, to create a lot big enough for a high-rise building).

☞ Exempt lands, owners, and land uses. Churches, often targeted by critics, are minor offenders. Cemeteries are major: they also include commercial ventures holding vast lands for future sale. Commercial or not, they consume more than their share of water, often at preferential rates. In industry-dependent Milwaukee, cemeteries preempt more space than all industry, which helps account for the city's 20% population decline since 1960. Public lands held by schools and the military tie up much of San Diego. New York City and Washington, DC, are notorious for their "free lists" of exempt lands. Once an agency acquires land it never again appears in the budget, so bureaucrats squander it.

☞ Homestead exemptions — widely abused in some states.

☞ Preferential underassessment of lands with low turnover. Extreme underassessment of lands that do not sell: corporate holdings; proprietary golf clubs; dynastic holdings; inherited lands.

☞ Rights of way. Assessors ignore monopoly power inherent in ROW, merely assessing ROW land on its value in the best alternative use

☞ Rail and utility adjunct landholdings (i.e. other than their ROW). These are state-assessed, not on local tax rolls; are assessed as acreage, usually, which means underassessment; anyway, taxes are passed on to ratepayers in the rate-regulation process. (Some examples: vast holdings by rails, e.g. 10% of Chicago; 5% of Milwaukee; vast Southern Pacific holding south of Market Street in San Francisco; hydrocarbon holdings by regulated utilities.)

☞ Discounts to large owners who have a policy of slow sales or leasing. (Such discounts are given to Oregon timber; to Appalachian coal; and many extractive resources. They are given to laggards in ecotones*.)

☞ Conventional reluctance to base assessments on speculative values, even when condemnation awards are so based.†

☞ Failure to assess land first, using maps (with building value as the "residual").

The national problem: IRS data

Many economists rely on data generated by the IRS, taken from tax returns, to tell them the sources of income in the US. This is an exercise in crediting bad data. The standard tax procedure of landlords is to deduct alleged "depreciation" from their net operating rents ("cash flow") to arrive at taxable rents. They accelerate depreciation enough, usually, to report little or no taxable rent. This is what the IRS then aggregates and reports as the sum of all rents.

---

* In biology, an ecotone is a region of transition between two biological communities. — *Ed.*

† c.f. the Supreme Court decision Lucas v. South Carolina Coastal Council. When land-use regulation took away a land parcel's development value, the Supreme Court upheld the "regulatory taking" of the parcel's entire value. Lucas was awarded the land's current value of $1.2 million, though he had bought it for $975,000. — *Ed.*

To accept such fiction as fact is inexcusable, but economists do it anyway. Their credulity lends their authority to the IRS, while the IRS "official" status helps legitimize the economists — mutual validation of mutual error, the curse of science.

When owner A has exhausted his tax "basis" by overdepreciating, he sells to B for a price well above the remaining basis. B then depreciates the same building all over again, then sells to C, and so on — each building is tax-depreciated several times during its economic life. In any given year, most income properties in the USA are being tax-depreciated, even though most have already been depreciated at least once.

In addition, all owners after the original builder are in a position to depreciate some of the land value, as well. This is because the owners control the "allocation of basis" between depreciable building and non-depreciable land. The IRS has no defense against successive owners who overallocate value to the depreciable building. Congress has never authorized the IRS to develop any in-house capacity to value land. The most the agency does, if it will not accept the word of the tax filer, is to look at allocations used by local assessors. These parties, in turn (with a few notable exceptions), underassess land relative to buildings, by using the "land-residual" method. This is partly to accommodate their local constituents — assessors are locally elected or appointed, and do not report to the IRS. A little math will tell you that to depreciate land just once is to achieve perpetual tax exemption. To depreciate it again and again is a continuing subsidy for holding land.

When A sells to B there is a large excess of the sales price over the remaining or "undepreciated" basis. This excess is, to be sure, taxable income. However, Congress has defined this kind of income as a "capital gain." Most rents, therefore, show up as capital gains. These, in turn, are subject to lower tax rates, deferral of tax, forgiveness at time of death and constant political pressure to lower rates to zero. These are known to every lawyer, accountant and Congressman, but apparently not to most economists, who lazily report from "official" data that rents are a very low fraction of national income.

In addition, the IRS reports nothing at all for the imputed income of owner-occupied lands, because this kind of non-cash income is not taxable. Todd Sinai and Joseph Gyourko of the Wharton School reported aggregate owner-occupied "house" values in the US in 1999 were $11.1 trillion. The annual rental value of that, figuring at 5%, would be roughly half a trillion dollars a year — quite a chunk to omit from the rental portion of national income. Such silent gains are also a form of income from land. To all that, many economists remain blind, dumb, and curiously incurious.

Sinai and Gyourko's treatment is superior to what one usually sees, because they make some effort to treat land separately. However, even they, like others, write of the imputed income of owner-occupied "housing," exclusively. That is doubly misleading. First, it emphasizes the building. That is wrong because the income properly imputable to the house *per se* is much less than its rent equivalent. The house requires constant expenses for upkeep, heating, maintenance and repairs, cleaning, painting, etc. The house also depreciates, physically. Those expenses and the depreciation must be deducted from the rental equivalent to get the net income.

The land does not depreciate physically, and so its rental equivalent is its net current income. Usually, it appreciates in value, and that annual increment is also a current income. So the lion's share of "imputed income of owner-occupied housing" is attributable to the land — but no one is saying so.

Second, the standard characterization of "house values" misleads by omitting vast lands beyond the narrowly defined "house" lot, which includes the land under the building and a little yard or curtilage. What about other lands held for the owners' personal enjoyment? No agency collects data on such lands and their values, but common observation tells us they are vast and valuable, and dominate values in many "rural" counties.

Another lode of error: "NIPA" accounts

The standard source of data on GNP and its components is the National Income and Product Account (NIPA), kept and published regularly by the US Department of Commerce. When it comes to rent, NIPA depends on the IRS figures, which thus are passed along to all students of economics as the "official" accounting. We have just seen how far from reality these data are.

NIPA is worse, in a way, because it explicitly excludes "capital gains" from National Income. That is, first the IRS converts rents into capital gains, and then NIPA banishes capital gains from GNP, National Income, and National Product. "Capital gains" is an artificial term, that includes all gains realized from the sale of what Congress defines at any time as "capital assets" — which include land and improvements, housing, common stock, growing timber, breeding herds (including race, show and riding horses), mineral and hydrocarbon reserves in the ground, and several other favorite holdings of the rich and well-connected. As we saw above, most commercial rents show up as capital gains, so that NIPA does not report them at all. Then along come highly visible economists, like Paul Samuelson, Robert Solow, Theodore Schultz, Edwin Mills and Jan Pen, to look up this datum, and declare that land rents, at no more than 5% of national income, cannot possibly support modern governments. This is unfortunate, and quite misleading.

Other prestigious sources of error

The Federal Reserve Board is ensnared in the same intellectual webs as the other agencies, so its nominal independence is wasted. Michael Hudson has dissected FRB methods, which resulted in reporting rents of income property far below reality. The *reductio ad absurdum* arrived when its clerks, evidently plodding "on automatic," duly reported that the rents of all the income property in the USA are negative. Someone in authority finally noticed, was embarrassed, and discontinued the report.

Many economists treat numbers from the National Bureau of Economic Research (NBER) as iconic. The press routinely cites their datings of US recessions and recoveries as "official." Many writers cite Raymond Goldsmith's estimates of United States land values, dating from 1955 and 1962, as "authoritative," because they carry the NBER imprimatur. Yet they do not bear examination, even for their times. They were generated as incidents to other work in an offhand and indefensible way.

It is not easy to retrace Goldsmith's steps; one must track interlocking footnotes from several sources. At the end of the trail, however, he simply takes residential land value as 13 percent of real estate value. The basis of this allocation is the share of land in the cost of houses insured by the Federal Housing Authority, which was about 20 percent. (He does not explain why he cut this down to 13 percent.) Goldsmith applies this basis to nonresidential real estate as well. As for corporate-held lands, he enters them at book value — an attitude that opened the door to an epidemic of corporate raiding. Goldsmith also seems to omit vacant lots and unsubdivided land.

These methods are not worthy of the faith with which several economists cite the results. FHA-insured houses are not typical. They tend to be new and on cheap land. Those not new are not very old — in 1967 the median age of insured existing homes was thirteen years. To apply such data to a typical American city, most of whose dwelling units in 1965 antedated 1920, was outlandish then, and even more outlandish today.

FHA clientele is lower middle class, which means the land share is low, land being both a consumer luxury and a rich man's hedge. Land share rises sharply with overall value. FHA data misses the high land share in enclaves of wealth such as Beverly Hills, Greenwich, Belvedere, Rancho Santa Fe, Palm Beach or Kenilworth.

The FHA is most active at the expanding fringe of cities. A basic fact of urban land economics is that the land share rises toward the center. In Manhattan, for example, the share of assessed land value has always been higher than in the other boroughs.

Applying a land fraction derived from residential data to commerce and industry is not believable. The land share is highest in retailing, the more so now that retailing entails vast parking areas. Gas stations and drive-ins of all kinds entail vast aprons for small buildings with short lives. Some retailers, such as auto dealerships and lumber yards, store their inventories outdoors. Many wholesalers and industries do the same: tank farms, railroad yards, utility easements, industrial reserves, dumps, salt beds, terminals, heaps of coal and salt and sulfur, and so on. In downtown Milwaukee, half the assessed value is land. In Manhattan, it is instructive to consider the Empire State Building. If ever a structure overdeveloped a site, this should be it. Yet in two transactions since 1950 the site was valued at one-third the total. One may infer what this implies of the whole island.

Anyone active in real estate would have caught Goldsmith's error. Yet it passed muster with the NBER, his publisher the Princeton University Press, and several learned academic reviewers. This is not a measure of their general incompetence, but of the extent to which academicians have walled themselves off from anything bearing on the realities of land values and rents. Goldsmith treated land carelessly, as a trivial side-issue, and his finding was ignored by everyone except those who needed to invoke an authority to trivialize land value.

Another Goldsmith error is to exclude subsoil assets. In cities overlying oil pools, like Huntington Beach, that would make a big difference. In most cities that may not matter, but it is symptomatic of how insouciantly Goldsmith handled the matter of land values.

Ernest Kurnow's work under Lincoln and Moley

Ernest Kurnow low-balled land and rent values in a chapter in *Theory and Measurement of Rent* by Keiper, Kurnow, Clark and Segal, 1961. In an introduction, the authors thank the Lincoln Foundation for financing their work, and go on to thank David Lincoln and Raymond Moley personally for intellectual guidance. Then, extraordinarily, they omit the standard disclaimer which absolves their advisors and takes full responsibility for their own work. This is a unique omission. *Res ipsa loquitur*: David Lincoln is speaking. That helps explain why researchers seeking full estimates of land values seek in vain at the Lincoln Institute of Land Policy.

Kurnow's basic source is tax assessments. He accepts their allocation of value between land and buildings. He admits that errors are possible, but dismisses them because "in all likelihood there is a tendency for such errors to cancel each other." We have seen how wrong and biased that is. He does not even correct for the assessment bias shown by sales-assessment ratios of Manvel's *Census of Governments*, nor for the greater degree of underassessment revealed by mapping of land values. He does not consider any of the 18 bulleted points shown above.

In short, the land portion of real estate value is much higher than standard modern sources show. One of many indications is that on most assessment rolls the value of old "junker" buildings, on the eve of demolition, is listed as higher than the land under them. It should be obvious that the old junker has no residual value: that is why it is being junked. Real estate people recognize this concept instantly. It is not obvious to everyone, everywhere, which helps keep it concealed, and provokes a lot of nostalgic resistance. People who make a virtue of recycling old cans and papers can be oblivious to the much higher social value of recycling old urban sites. Many of these old "junkers" even appear sound and valuable, as in enclaves of high values like Winnetka, Illinois, or Beverly Hills, California, but suffer from "locational obsolescence," which is the key concept. That means the growing value of the underlying site for recycling has cannibalized the residual building value.

Most modern economists who look into these matters rely upon the standard sources I've listed here, mindless (or perhaps even glad) of their downward biases. Young students are intimidated and awed, or at least impressed and convinced, by the "official-looking" auspices of the standard sources.

II. Broadening the concepts of land and its rent

Rents tappable by variable charges

The term "single tax" has been unfortunate in helping to perpetuate a narrow fixation on property taxes; as a result, even advocates of land value taxation tend to underestimate the revenue potential from rents. Many lands and resources that yield rents are not observed or measured in traditional real estate markets. There is a new realization that "taxes on rent" are much broader than the traditional land value tax.

As esteemed a Georgist as William Vickrey[*] often pronounced the prime virtue of land value taxes to be that they are a lump sum, invariant with production or sales. He thus identified them solely as property taxes, and not any variable charge like a severance tax on withdrawing water or oil, a parking fee, a gas tax, or a bridge toll (though he favored all of these, for what he saw as other reasons). He did not see the corporate income tax (which he opposed) as being in part a rent tax. It is a cliché of economics texts to class land taxes together with poll taxes as having the peculiar virtue of not being based on any variable input or output. In this mindset, there are no differences worth mentioning between poll taxes and land taxes — an instance of tunnel-vision that would be surprising in any discipline except, alas, modern economics.

Dick Netzer[†] would substitute "a family of user charges" for taxes on buildings. So strong is the "single-tax" stereotype, though, that not even Netzer thought to include user charges as part of land revenues. Then there are mineral revenues from severance taxes and/or royalties. These are already so great that some polities get much, or

---

[*] Vickrey, 1914-1996, was an ardent Georgist professor of economics and Nobel Laureate, famous for his work on taxing unrealized capital gains.

[†] Netzer, 1929-2008, was a professor of economics who specialized in municipal finance issues, and advised the New York City government during its celebrated financial troubles in the 1970s.

even most of their revenues therefrom. And yet the confining "single tax" tradition is so strong that Netzer does not include mineral revenues among land-based taxes — not even in the rents tapped by oil-rich Norway and other North Sea nations. It is a major omission. In one year the mere increase in the value of Norway's undersea reserves exceeded its entire national income.

Variable charges, such as those on road crowding, water withdrawals from surface and underground sources, minerals extraction, air and water pollution, spectrum use, fish catches, billboards, etc., are major additions to land revenues. California, a major oil-producing state, does not even have a severance tax, not even a token. In the fiscal crisis of 2003, with 136 or so candidates running for Governor, only one (Arianna Huffington) even mentioned it, so total is the mental blackout in the state.

If we seek to implement a program of securing the universal right to natural opportunities via the public capture of land rents, then products that cause damage, anti-social behavior and inflated demand for publicly-subsidized medical care may reasonably be taxed. Some examples:

☞ Our most lucrative agricultural industry, marijuana, would provide high tax yields, should we decide to legalize it instead of trying vainly to suppress it. We would save the high public costs of the "narcocracy," the counter-industry that depends on drug-users for its very existence. We would save a substantial fraction of the money spent on jails and warding: a splendid example of trading "Negabucks for Megabucks."

☞ Graffiti might be administratively difficult to tax, but what about billboards? These are merely legalized graffiti with social standing. Anyone who doubts the reality of visual pollution might shed all doubts by driving through Vermont, a state that outlaws billboards. The aesthetic and cultural differences are hard to miss.

☞ Superior resources should bear an extraction charge. In 1984 a geothermal source near Santa Rosa went for $350 million from Occidental Petroleum to a Kuwaiti owner, as part of the trend toward the Banana Republic-ization of this highly rentable state.

☞ Taxing air and water polluters by levying "effluent charges" won the favor of the economists dominant in the 1960s. The reasoning was pure Georgism: make them pay for preempting publicly owned air.

☞ Taxing pollution surrogates (such as the pesticides that later run unpredictably off of fields) is also popular, especially to deal with non-point pollution that does not lend itself to effluent charges. The policy has its limits, but is part of any program to combat nonpoint pollution.

Capturing rent via income taxation

The income tax base includes income from land. For this we have to thank a few Georgist Congressmen of 1894 who got land included in the base of the income tax which Congress enacted then. In Pollock v. Farmers' Loan and Trust Co., (1894), the Supreme Court threw out the whole law for that specific reason; the 16th Amendment of 1913 was necessary, basically, to let land income be included in the base.

Corporate income was successfully taxed from 1909, before the 16th Amendment, as an excise tax on the privilege of doing business as a corporation. "The excise tax used net income as a measure of the privilege of corporate business practice."* The legalistic circumlocution suggests how creative lawyers can implement what Congress really wants. Someday another text might read "The excise tax used land value as a measure of the privilege of holding title to natural resources." Indeed, the Ralston-Nolan Bill of 1920, and the Keller Bill of 1924, used exactly such language as the constitutional basis for imposing a national 1% charge on holding title to land.

But that may not even be necessary now. State legislatures,

---

* Bernard Herber, *Modern Public Finance*, p. 190.

like Congress, have nearly complete control and discretion over what kinds of income to include or exclude from the income tax base. They have abandoned most of their discretion by piggybacking on Federal laws, but they have not abandoned all of it, and they could take it all back.

The income tax can be converted into a tax on land income in two steps. The first one is surpassingly simple: exempt wage and salary income from the tax. One could tiptoe up on this by raising the earned income exemption, the standard deduction, personal exemptions, etc. Workers paying the social security tax should be allowed to deduct it from taxable income. Raise the rates on what remains of the income tax base, which would now be mostly property income. If that seems shocking or radical, recall that from 1913 to 1941 (before withholding, and the explosion of the FICA deduction) most wage and salary income was in fact exempt. What is really shocking and radical is the massive shift of tax burden off of property income and onto wage and salary income, a shift that has perverted the whole notion of income taxation as originally adopted in 1913.

The second step is to remove capital income from the base. This is harder to understand, but easier to accomplish because it has already been done in part. The present tax law includes several devices designed to lower or effectively eliminate any tax on the income from capital. Basically, this is done by letting investors write off what they invest at or near the time they invest it. The investment tax credit (ITC) even goes farther and lets them write off more than they invest.

"Expensing" of certain capital investments means writing them off 100% in the year made. Accelerated depreciation is a substantial move in the same direction. Even straight-line depreciation is really accelerated compared to the true depreciation paths of durable capital, especially when coupled with the use of tax lives which are much shorter than economic lives of durable capital items.

None of those devices apply to land, however, because land is not depreciable. That is again thanks to generations of Georgists, starting with those in the Progressive movement when the income tax was shaped. Who else would keep officials conscious that land is different? Standard-brand academic economists keep pushing the notion that land is just a form of capital.

To convert the tax fully to land, then, we need only complete step two by allowing universal expensing of all new investments. Voila!

At the same time we must plug many loopholes designed especially for land income. One of these is depreciating land, even though land does not wear out. This is illegal, strictly speaking, but it is often winked at in practice when old buildings are depreciated from their purchase price by new buyers.

Many will object that the income tax only hits realized income from land, and exempts the holder who neglects or under-utilizes land. True enough — but consider the behavior of private landlords and tenants. They often prefer arrangements that share risks and returns, like the income tax, instead of fixed cash rents that resemble the property tax. The cases are not perfectly analogous in all particulars, but suggestive.

It seems clear that, should a legislature wish to go further in this good direction, it could define "land income" as a fixed proportion of land value, regardless of use. Plenty of economists would come forth to testify that that is a reasonable definition.

Substituting taxes for subsidies to promote conservation

Here is a high potential to turn "Negabucks into Megabucks" for the treasury. For generations, we have subsidized landowners to withdraw water. The benefits of the subsidy have gone roughly in proportion to the area of irrigable land owned. As a result, water is maldistributed, underpriced and wasted. Today, for a change, there is support (at least intellectually) for a groundwater extraction charge, purely as a conservation and efficiency measure, and to obviate megabuck "rescue" projects. However, if we can wrench our mindsets away from the crazy tradition of subsidizing waste and maldistribution, there is also great revenue potential in water. In an arid land, water is life. Some, perhaps much, of the land rent now imputing to fee simple lands can be transferred to the holders of water, simply by raising its price.

Why should we want to transfer the burden to the holders of water? Because a state's water belongs to its people. A license to withdraw the people's water is not real property (and thus not sheltered by Prop 13). The State can serve free market efficiency and raise revenue in one stroke by putting a charge on water withdrawals. Such a charge would expedite the powerful current movement to market water.

An economic charge should of course be geared to the economic value (locational, mainly) of waters. Groundwater has been mentioned. Surface water could bear higher charges because it is already at the surface with no pumping. This charge might be called a "tax," or a rental for state property, as legalism and politics may require. The charge should cover not just active withdrawals, but "dog-in-the-manger" licenses to block withdrawals by others. Value-data to help set a proper charge would come from the proposed free market in tradable water licenses.

Unearned increments as current rents

There is a swelling of "capital" gains (mostly land gains, actually) as a component of income. In this case there is no corresponding realization among economists or the public that capital gains on land are eminently taxable. On the contrary, as gains grow so do the wealth and political power of the movement to untax them. So much greater, then, is the need for objective economists to establish the taxability of capital gains. Unrealized gains can be taxed as they accrue, without disincentive effects or administrative nightmares, and economists need to estimate the new revenue potential that now largely escapes taxation.

Capital gains as a revenue source can be quite unstable.

California's recent (2003) fiscal bind illustrates the problem. This should not be taken to be a drawback of the present proposal, however, for the proposal here differs from the current income tax on capital gains in several ways.

My proposed tax is focused on unearned increments to land values. Current income taxes include gains from a variety of other sources, like building up a new business. During the dot.com boom, it was this last element that was most unstable.

My proposal is to tax land-value gains as they accrue, rather than upon sale. A property tax based on the market value of "ripening" land automatically taxes the current accrual, because both are proportional to the current market value. During a land boom and bust, land taxes are a strong stabilizing factor.

My proposed tax excludes gains on common stocks.

Variant kinds of land resources, hitherto neglected or not classed, or only recently classed with land, show great revenue potential. Some examples are the radio spectrum; telecom relay sites; slots in geosynchronous orbit; Pigovian taxes to curtail overuse and pollution of common airs and waters, while also raising revenue. (Many academicians, sadly, are dragging their feet and making themselves part of the problem by bickering over whether this is possible.)

Uncapping the tax rate on land

The standard reasons for avoiding high tax rates, and spreading low rates of taxation around to many sources, do not apply to land:

☞ The base is not erodable (tax capitalization is not erosion)

☞ There is no taxable event, hence no Laffer Effect or Excess Burden (except, as discussed above, in cases of extraction charges — where the slow-down effect is deliberate, for conservation reasons).

☞ Base is highly concentrated, making the tax progressive in impact. The tax is not shifted, so ultimate incidence is same as impact. Progressivity minimizes the number of true hardship cases, and hence the cost of relieving them.

☞ The tax encourages *both* saving and investing, leveling them upwards, the macroeconomist's dream.

☞ The tax base is the after-tax value of land, making the real rate much lower than the apparent rate.

☞ Using the tax to obviate other taxes raises the tax base via the ATCOR effect (see part III).

☞ The tax fosters better allocation of the tax base, raising its taxable capacity.

☞ The tax hits absentee owners of land, without discouraging the inflow of capital. This creates a strong local multiplier effect.

Ownership of wealth generally, and land and capital gains particularly, are highly concentrated. They are much more concentrated than incomes from productive labor, and increasingly so. Thus, taxes based on land rents and values are progressive in their impact and incidence, at the same time they are pro-incentive in their allocative effects. This combination of virtues is unique. It belies the cliché that governments must always choose between equity and efficiency in taxation. It makes it possible to raise tax rates to high levels without either stifling good incentives or embracing regressivity. This greatly enhances the revenue potential of such taxes.

The unseen reservoir of high internal valuations and holdout prices

Observed land markets understate the value of land to most landowners. These owners' internal valuations are above the observed market: that is why they do not offer to sell. In most land markets, annual turnover is 5% or less. Assessors take that sample to estimate the value of the whole. The other 95% of landowners in effect "sell" or "rent" to themselves each year. How accurately does that 5% sample the entire invisible "market" for land? Many owners routinely declare "Get away from my door; I will not sell for any price."

Modern environmental economics has spawned the discipline of "contingent valuation" to appraise damages to resources that seldom pass through markets. It turns out there is a major difference between WTP values (what are Willing To Pay, i.e., for cleaner air) and WTA values (what payment you are Willing To Accept to let me pollute your clean air). WTA >> WTP. Where there are market dealings to observe, they are based on WTP values, so the observed market conceals WTA values, which are much higher than the active, visible "market." The "willing seller" concept is mostly fictional: it is the "motivated seller" who makes the market — the observed market, that is. Most sales are "forced" to some degree. Other owners hold out for much higher prices.

Status-quo theory is shaken to the roots by survey findings that WTA >> WTP. If we acknowledge the common birthright to a clean environment, then you can't pollute anyone's air or water, because the victims own it. They can be as unreasonable as any great landlord. This explains why theorists are so busily trying to plug the dike. It was 1974 when a survey first showed WTA >> WTP, "in contradiction to received theory." This sent dozens of professors and think-tankers scurrying to torture data and logic until they confessed otherwise, to save Coase and Stigler. They have succeeded in keeping the mass of economists in denial on the matter, so economists don't even see its implications.

The meaning for tax policy is that there is scope for substantially raising tax rates on land without flooding the market with distress sellers. That will disappoint those (including myself) who see land taxes as a means to cheapen land for new buyers. That goal will take high tax rates; but *en route* to the goal (and also afterward) we can raise great revenues, which is the present point.

The flipside of high internal valuations by owners is that roughly one third of American families are renters. Their internal valuations of what they rent are obviously lower than the market value of these or comparable quarters.

III. ATCOR (All Taxes Come Out of Rents)

When we lower taxes, the revenue base is not lost, but shifted to land rents and values, which can then yield more taxes. This is most obvious with taxes on buildings. When we exempt buildings, and raise tax rates on the land under them, we are still taxing the same real estate; we are just taxing it in a different way. We will show that this "different way" actually raises the revenue capacity of real estate by a large factor. There is much recent historical experience with exempting buildings from the property tax, in whole or part. It has shown that builders offer more for land, and sellers demand more, when the new buildings are to be untaxed. The effect on revenue is the same as taxing prospective new buildings before they are even built, even though the new buildings are not to be taxed at all.

Land value is what the bare land would sell for. It is specifically and immediately most sensitive to taxes on new buildings, and on land sales, as well as to new and more stringent building code requirements or zoning that often discriminate against new buildings. Where new buildings are "coded" more severely than old, it enhances the value of the old land/building packages. This premium should be considered part of land value, and taxable as such.

We have numerous historical experiences with exempting buildings leading to land booms: New York City 1922-33, Western Canada, Hong Kong, Taiwan, Australia, South Africa, San Francisco after the fire, Chicago after the fire, California Irrigation Districts, Cleveland 1903-20, Toledo, Detroit, Portland, Seattle, Houston, San Diego.

Familiar micro cases

The general principle that tax cuts shift to higher rents is, in many ways, like the forest: too ubiquitous for most to see clearly. But here are a few of the trees:

☞ Lowering corporate income tax rates raises stock markets.

☞ Lowering the income tax rate on capital gains has doubtless contributed to the following runup in land prices.

☞ Private commercial rents in leases are usually multipartite. A lower share of gross revenues is traded off for a higher fixed rent, or vice versa. It's like the law of conservation of energy in physics: everything must be accounted for, and for every action there is an equal and opposite reaction. Commercial rents in retailing usually contain at least two elements: 1) a fixed monthly rent and 2) a share of sales (or sometimes of profits). If the rate in element (2) is higher, then element (1) will be lower, to compensate. Reports by the city-owned Port of Milwaukee show how they handle industrial leases the same way.

☞ Payroll taxes and disincentive kinds of business taxes make firms leave states, lowering demand for land. This does not, of course, discourage the minority of business activity that does not contribute to production; Walter Rybeck[*] has sagely suggested that we distinguish two functions of "business:" wealth-creating and resource-holding. A good tax system will make people pay for simply holding resources, but not for creating wealth.

The Resource Curse effect

Economists and historians have noticed that nations and regions that are rich in natural resources to export often lag in manufacturing. This is often now called "The Dutch Disease," although obviously they did not catch it until modern times, with the oil and natural gas booms. These prized exportable items raised the value of the guilder, making Dutch manufactures cost foreigners more, and letting Dutch consumers import competing foreign products. Canada exports lumber and energy products to the same effect; so does Alaska, which also collects great federal largesse, military and porkbarrel. Canada taps into resource revenues to lower

---

[*] Journalist and government advisor Rybeck directs the Center for Public Dialogue, and is the author of *Re-solving the Economic Puzzle* (2012)

national taxes; Alaska, to lower other State taxes and distribute a social dividend to each resident. Thus, resource rents help raise other land values.

Utility-rate effect

Lower rates mean higher land values. During the Progressive Era, rapid growth of cities called for providing costly utilities and transit on a new and massive scale. Many big-city mayors, some directly instructed by Tom L. Johnson of Cleveland, saw that providing these services raised land values, which could be taxed to pay for them. Private franchisees saw they could profit by squeezing monopoly profits from the franchises. It became a running battle.

The economics profession lagged in responding. A number of professors were removed from leading universities after writing or speaking too openly against the franchises (Tom Johnson hired one of them, Edward Bemis, to advise him on rate regulation). Rich franchisees, after all, might help endow universities as Chicago traction magnate Charles Yerkes did with his observatory. But in 1938 Professor Harold Hotelling of Columbia drew the point sharply in a leading article in the obscurely statistical journal *Econometrica*. He was followed over time by a school of thinkers who favor "Marginal-cost pricing," which often means lowering user rates on mass transit and utilities, making up the deficits by taxing the benefited lands. Theorist Abba Lerner even tried to squeeze all of economics into what he called "The Rule"— set price equal to marginal cost.

The logic of ATCOR

The thesis that all taxes are shifted to landowners follows logically from two premises. One, after-tax interest rates are determined by world markets. The local supply of capital is perfectly elastic at a fixed, after-tax rate. Two, labor's wages have been reduced to so low a level that they cannot bear any more tax burden. Anyone may test the premises by observation.

If there are unemployed workers, then the supply of "work" (as opposed to "labor," defined as so many warm bodies) is highly elastic. When we find work for the unemployed and underemployed, labor gains without costing land or capital anything at all. Even better, in fact, labor gains while benefiting other taxpayers, because of lower dole costs, lower crime costs, etc. The enhanced psychic benefit of universal job security is also worth a lot (although not in direct money). In the era when Keynesianism was in flower, many alleged that the social cost of putting the unemployed to work is zero.

It is likely that real wage rates would rise, as more-efficient land use increased demand for labor and lowered product prices. Compact settlement would create new rents via the synergies that are not aborted by scatter. This was the theme of *Progress and Poverty*, and the primary goal of Henry George's reforms. True, that was before we had heavy payroll and income taxes on labor. In real terms, though, the outcome is the same: it is likely that the abolition of such taxes would let after-tax wage rates rise, even while before-tax wage rates remain the same, or fall. To the extent that this process diminished, if it did, the overall public-revenue potential of land, few would call it a calamity.

Capital supply is elastic

Most economists assume this, emphasizing world markets, rapid transfers, arbitrage. However (and in addition), even in small closed economies, there is underemployed capital, just like labor. This is because the return is held down by taxation. So it goes into untaxed consumer goods, and tax-exempt forms of capital, like housing, foundations, government works or personal property. When all uses of capital are untaxed, these forms would be placed on equal footing with higher-yield opportunities. From this would spring a large supply — voila! elasticity in the supply of capital. George recognized this, although he had his own way of expressing it. He did not regard consumer capital as being "really" capital (as it was not actively being used in production), but he did observe people living on it while they produced other capital. During World War II we experienced a vivid example of how people can draw down consumer capital to meet an emergency need.

Logic and experience both overwhelmingly support the idea of ATCOR. To summarize: the revenue capacity of land, when it is substituted for other tax bases, is comparable to current revenues. Owing to efficiency effects, and renewal effects, it may well be higher. The major reservation is that the supply of labor is not totally elastic, so some of the revenue gains may be "lost" in higher wage rates, but higher wage rates are socially desirable, and serve to lower many public costs as for welfare, policing and jailing, aggressive military spending, make-work projects, etc.

Multiplier effect of taxing absentee owners

Transferring rents from them to our fisc, and spending the proceeds locally, improves the state economic base and balance of payments. It is alleged that we must avoid taxing absentees, because they will remove their capital from our state, but they cannot remove their land. The only way they can remove oil and gas is by producing them. The present owners of most of our oil and gas became so by acquiring it from existing local owners and producers, so it is hard to argue they ever did bring capital into the state. It is easy to argue, however, that a democratic sovereign state reports to and is responsible to the resident electors, not absentee owners. It is easy to argue that the quality of life is worsened when absentee owners displace local owners and turn local people into tenants. There is no social value in encouraging absentees.

A high percentage of real property is owned from out of state and even out of the country. The percentage is much higher than we may think. It is not just Japanese banks and the Arabs in Beverly Hills. It is corporate-held property which comprises almost half the real estate tax base. If we assume that California's share of the stockholders equals its share of the national population, then ninety per cent of this property is absentee-owned; the percentage may be higher because many of these are multinational corporations with multinational owners.

There is a curious silence on the matter. Some critics of capping the property tax rate talk about "business" securing the lion's share of benefits. No one seems to have seized on the fact that half the taxable property in California is owned by people who do not vote in the state, and do not spend their income in the state. Here is one instance where localism (which can be ugly, as we know) may be harnessed to help create a more healthy society. The purpose of democracy is to represent the electorate, not the absentee who stands between the resident and the resources of his homeland.

California's legislative analyst, William Hamm, estimated in 1978 that over fifty per cent of the value of taxable property in California was absentee-owned. This is such a bold, bare, and enormous fact it is hard to believe that Californians could be misled into resisting the urge to levy taxes on all this foreign wealth. They may be put off by the argument that they need to attract outside capital, but that carries no weight when considering the large percentage of this property which is land value.

Some half of any reduction in California property taxes leaks to out-of-state owners. Nor is this the only leakage. Net federal income tax payments have risen because sales and nuisance taxes raised to replace lost property taxes are not deductible. Sales of local general obligation bonds have stopped and will stay stopped. Revenue bonds are sold instead, with higher interest rates. Fire insurance rates must rise. And private spending substituted for public spending will have a higher propensity to import. Public spending goes for policemen, firemen, teachers, local contractors, and so on.

This substantial leakage of economic base results in multiple declines in state income. One drastic example of this is offshore oil and gas, which is outside state sovereignty and escapes all state and local taxation. One result is unbalanced state hostility to offshore leasing, for the locals suffer the degradation without sharing the gains. Some provision for state sharing in offshore revenues seems indicated.

The picture so far

In this article we have discussed fourteen new elements of land's taxable capacity. Previous estimates of rent and land values have been narrowly limited to a fraction of the whole, thus giving an entirely false impression that the tax capacity is similarly narrow. We are adding the following elements to the traditional narrow "single tax" base:

☞ Correcting omissions and understatements in standard data sources

☞ Updating ancient sources that use obsolete low values

☞ Raising the Land Fraction of Real Estate Values

☞ Adding rents that are best taxed by use of variable excises

☞ Adding rents taxable by income taxes

☞ Substituting taxes for subsidies to foster conservation

☞ Adding current unearned increments as part of ongoing rent

☞ Adding previously invisible and undervalued resources to the tax base

☞ Adding lands held under variant forms of tenure

☞ Adding rents that are now dissipated (as by urban blight and sprawl), but need not be

☞ Noting the feasibility of much higher tax rates on a base that is both non-erosive, and concentrated in ownership

☞ Noting the great mass of holdout prices (WTA values) exceed visible market prices (WTP values) by a large factor

☞ Adding the revenue from most existing taxes to the potential land tax base, on the ATCOR principle

☞ Multiplier effect of taxing absentee landowners

Any one of those Fourteen Elements indicates a significantly higher land tax base than economists commonly perceive today. Taken together, they are overwhelming, and cast an entirely new light on this subject.

One final rent-raising factor: mortgage interest as land rent

Here is one further supplement to the land rent tax base, which I am not counting among the basic fourteen because it involves novel thinking, and is fraught with controversy, which might divert us too much from the main chance.

One kind of paper is systematically recorded at the county level: mortgages, or deeds of trust. It is administratively feasible to put these into the property tax base, as Professor Don Hagman kept urging. But is it desirable? A tax on mortgages would be mostly shifted to borrowers in the form of higher interest rates, the supply of mortgage funds being highly elastic. Thus, to tax mortgages is indirectly to tax real estate.

It is widely assumed that cheap long term credit is essential to let most people buy real estate. Unfortunately that reasoning overlooks the nature of land values, which makes it circular. The main effect of long term loans has been to inflate land prices, *creating the very problem it offsets*. It is a treadmill effect, like keeping up with the Joneses.

It must be conceded that holders of existing mortgages would suffer. But someone suffers with any change of tax or other public policy; there are always winners and losers. It is a risk all investors take knowingly. Phasing-in is possible, and it should be remembered that in a Georgist tax shift, most holders of mortgages would be relieved of some or all of the income-tax burden they currently endure. (Another benefit of including mortgages in the property tax base is to counter the argument that the property tax discriminates against equity holders of real estate. Many have questioned the fairness of focusing taxes on the person with 5% equity in a parcel, while exempting his bank.)

Would new lending be discouraged? Yes, at the margins. The

most sensitive margin is one which most people would not perceive at first, that is the margin of durability or longevity. The more deferred the benefit of an investment, the more interest-sensitive is its present value. But, is that bad? We are conditioned to answer "yes," but as an economist, I doubt it. The financial system will adapt by basing loans less on land collateral, and more on buildings, inventories, accounts receivable, crops, personal reputation, and appraisal of specific projects. This is more labor-intensive banking, and less capital-intensive. Untaxing labor, as proposed herein, makes this more feasible. On balance this will help stabilize the financial system, whose worst fiascos, like the South Sea Bubble of 1720, the world banking collapse of 1932, the American Savings-and-Loan debacle of 1987-91, the Japanese collapse after 1992, and, of course, the Great Crash of 2008 have resulted from speculative loans on land.

Rent as revenue: quantity and quality

I hope that this brief survey has demonstrated land's suitability as a tax base in terms of quantity. It is eminently suitable in terms of quality as well. The macro-economic benefits are deep, wide, high, and temporal. To produce the added goods the owner invests more capital and hires more labor, or sells parcels to laborers wanting to go into business on their own. The newly employed workers earn income to buy the newly produced goods and services. Here is supply-side economics coupled with demand-side economics. The conventional left-wing objections to Say's Law do not apply here, because we are untaxing capital at the same time, and raising investment opportunities.[*] We are financing government to provide needed infrastructure to develop new lands, or redevelop brownfield lands, to open new investment opportunities for private capital. The conventional right-wing objection that capital

---

[*] The law of Jean-Baptiste Say (1767–1832) has been paraphrased as "Supply creates its own demand." It has been argued that if there is excessive saving in the economy, there can be a glut of products that will not find buyers. — *Ed.*

is limited does not apply, either, because we are stimulating saving, stimulating import of capital, and raising turnover of capital. (Turnover raises the ratio of income-creating investing to capital.) It is the macro-economist's dream, leveling upwards while balancing supply and demand, saving and investing.

— Adapted from "The Hidden Taxable Capacity of Land: Enough and to Spare." International Journal of Social Economics, *Vol 36, No. 4, 2009*

The Danger of Favoring Capital over Labor

———⟫◦⟪———

Henry George's declared aim in *Progress and Poverty*, and in his life, was to raise wages. "Why do wages tend to a minimum which will give but a bare living?" George declared the original War on Poverty; he kicked off the original agitation for Full Employment. He was overtly egalitarian: he dedicated *Progress and Poverty* to those who see "the vice and misery that spring from the unequal distribution of wealth..." He began with concern for labor, tenants, the unemployed, the impoverished, the "mudsills of society." He did not treat them as a special case, though, to be treated with targeted programs. Rather, he saw the whole wage structure — everyone's wage and salary — as a pyramid based on the wages of unskilled labor.

George's thought then led him along a twisting path. Had there been a wage tax in his day he would surely have fought it, but there was not. His thought led him to identify capital with labor, and thus to champion untaxing buildings, machinery, inventories, and other forms of capital, which he virtually equated with the labor that produced them.

There were no retail sales taxes to fight then (they burgeoned after 1932), but there were other taxes on consumption, and on commerce, both internal and external. Consistently, he also fought them. Untaxing commerce was an end in itself, but even more it was a means to deny the revenues to governments, so they must raise revenues by taxing land values instead. The Founding Fathers, led by James Monroe, had achieved something of the same end, in part, by forbidding states to tax interstate commerce, forcing them back on property taxation. George aimed to reinforce that outcome, and extend it to the Federal level as well.

George did not champion land taxes for merely being "neutral" (which is about the most that neoclassical economists will grudgingly concede). George saw land taxes as a positive good, a way to overcome the tendency of free markets in land, beset by speculation, to keep land from full economical use. He saw that not as a little glitch in the land market, but as driving down labor's marginal productivity and wages. He saw it, by the same reasoning, driving down the marginal productivity of capital, and rates of return to investors.

He saw "free trade in land," without land taxation, as a chimerical policy, the brood of *a priori* dogmatism, uninformed by observation. Human experience with free trade in land, like the mid-19th century English/Irish experiment with it, had shown that such markets lead to "unequal distribution of wealth and privilege" — the very ills that he dedicated *Progress and Poverty* to curing.

His emphasis on untaxing buildings, however, meant that by the end of his life he had shed many of his original allies, the socialists and unionists, and become more the candidate of small businessmen and small homeowners. Many of these were moved by short term and petty self-interest of a kind too niggling, too bourgeois, and often mean-spirited, to coexist in harmony with the spiritual and idealistic pro-labor forces that George had evoked earlier. His dedication to national politics, and free trade, also repelled his crowd-stirring spiritual ally, the popular Catholic rebel, Fr. Edward McGlynn.*

---

* Rev. McGlynn, 1837-1900, was a Catholic priest and social reformer. He supported Henry George's run for mayor of New York in 1886, and with

George aimed at national goals. He originally got into New York City politics opportunistically. That was his greatest political success, in 1886, but thereafter he aimed for State office, failing. The times changed after the Haymarket Riot of 1886, and economic recovery weakened the demand for reform. George's political alliance broke up. After that, in 1894, he coached a team of six Congressmen, associated with the Populist Party, who forced land taxation into the income tax act of that year. The six also supported his free trade position, whose strategic end was to force Washington to tax property in some manner, by denying the treasury its major source of revenue, the tariff. This strategy didn't get far until 1913, after George's death.

George's national interest was inherent in the thesis of *Progress and Poverty*. In its preface, he denies the possibility of achieving his goals by merely local action. Unemployment and hard times "can hardly be accounted for by local causes." Where the conditions of material progress are most fully realized "we find the deepest poverty... and the most of enforced idleness." "Social difficulties... do not arise from local circumstances, but are... engendered by progress itself."

"When San Francisco reaches the point where New York now is, who can doubt that there will also be ragged and bare-footed children on her streets?" Score one for "The Prophet of San Francisco."† He even understated his case. Today in San Francisco it is ragged, barefooted and homeless adults sleeping in her parks and doorways, and under her bridges, seeking escape in drugs, hard by the most expensive and luxurious housing in the USA.

How, then, did George's movement segue into a movement

George formed the popular "Anti-Poverty Society. Summoned to Rome in 1887 to explain his social-reform efforts, McGlynn refused to go, and was excommunicated. In 1892 he wrote a doctrinal statement, which was an exposition of George's "single-tax" philosophy. This was deemed not to contradict Catholic teaching, and McGlynn was reinstated to the priesthood. — *Ed.*

† This was the title of a biography of George by Louis F. Post, Chicago journalist and ardent single taxer, who served as Assistant Secretary of Labor in the administration of Woodrow Wilson. — *Ed.*

mainly to untax buildings, one town at a time? There have been many factors at work, but I focus here on one, of paramount importance: George's identifying capital with labor. We criticize neoclassical economists for using "two-factor" thinking, fusing capital with land; but George had his own kind of two-factorism, fusing capital with labor. Thus, many Georgists channel their energies into untaxing capital. Some of them may believe, if only subconsciously, that untaxing capital is the same as untaxing labor, and reaches George's goals.

How did George lay the groundwork for that? Few teachers in the Henry George Schools, or in universities either, think highly of *Progress and Poverty's* Book I on capital, or Book III, Chapter III, "Interest and the Cause of Interest." These, if read too closely, are embarrassments. Only his spritely writing style, filled with illustrations and examples from George's colorful life, let his early readers survive them and get through to the meat of his book. One intelligent and influential critic, Thomas Henry Huxley, apparently read no further than Book I, and rejected all of George on the grounds that George simply did not understand capital and interest very well. On this point (but not otherwise), Huxley was right. What little we know about the bankruptcy of George's newspaper in San Francisco suggests he did not manage capital well, and overextended himself. Most of my readers know that I admire and laud George, and intend no cheap shot or nasty *ad hominem*. It is just prudent to be aware of weaknesses, even of those whom we venerate.

George's attitude toward capital is insouciant. At one point he says the economy, like an organism, "secretes, as it were," the needed amount of capital. This is cavalier, and inconsistent with his later activism in the cause of untaxing buildings (to help the economic organism secrete more capital). At another point he has the path between production and consumption like "a curved pipe filled with water. If a quantity of water is poured in at one end, a like quantity is released at the other. It is not identically the same water, but is its equivalent. And so (laborers) put in as they take out — they receive in... wages but the produce of their own labor."

That is the "Fallacy of the Costless Inventory." It is like saying that planting a seedling douglas fir produces the 60-year old tree, if the firm harvests one at the same time. It is like saying students go through college instantly and at no cost, because a freshman enters for every senior who graduates.

The core fallacy, one with a strangely Marxian provenance, is George's repeated insistence that labor — and only labor — is what creates capital. In fact, we form capital by consuming less than income — by saving, that is — and investing a like amount. The income may come from rent or interest, not just from labor; and the capital that is produced contains contributions of value from all three factors. Most of the saving comes, and probably always has come, from property income: rent, interest, and business profits (which are mostly rent and interest). A lot of capital, like mature timber, contains more "stored-up rent" than stored-up labor. It also contains a high fraction of "stored-up capital." * I draw three lessons from this.

1. George never supplied, and we still do not have, a true "three-factor economics." Georgist economics is just as guilty of "two-factorism" as is neo-classical economics. They fuse capital with land; we fuse it with labor. Georgist theorists need to supply a complete theory, and Georgists need to learn it and teach it and use it. Capital is truly a third factor of production, with its own complexities and meanings.

2. We must not promote or tolerate untaxing capital more than we untax labor. That is what has happened with the personal income tax, creating a huge bias toward substituting capital for labor. Local zoning policies reinforce this powerfully, too, as most localities reserve land for capital-intensive uses in preference

---

* Those wanting to pursue this in depth will find the mathematics worked out in the appendix to this writer's "Toward Full Employment with Limited Land and Capital," a chapter in Arthur Lynn, Jr. (ed.), *Property Taxation, Land Use and Public Policy*. Madison: Univ. of Wisconsin Press, 1976, pp. 99-166.

to labor-intensive uses.

In one apocalyptic passage, anticipating Karel Capek (author of *Rossum's Universal Robots*), George foresees and warns against this tendency (bk. V, chp. 3). Citing the use of farm machinery in wheat fields, and its displacement of labor, he says we cannot "assign any limits to the increase of rent, short of the whole produce. ... (This is) *the final goal toward which the whole civilized world is hastening*" (my emphasis). Scary Mary! His readers must have sat up and taken notice at this point. It is strange that he drops such a powerful bomb in the middle of a paragraph, and does not make it the center of his thesis from there on, but there it lies. He does not, like Capek, have the robots take over the world and eliminate mankind. Rather, the landowners do, and interest falls to zero, as wages do. Implicitly, he seems to have "labor-saving inventions" also save capital, so little but land is needed in production. I cannot unravel all his thinking. The point is, though, that at one point, at least, he saw the danger in substituting capital for labor, and he saw it even in the absence of the kinds of bias now lodged in the Internal Revenue Code. As American jobs disappear overseas, it behooves us to see it, too.

3. George taught that to raise wages and end poverty we must act at the national level: local action alone is not enough. This is a challenge to keep us busy the rest of our lives. [*]

---

[*] On the point, I modestly refer you to my article, "A Cannan Hits the Mark," in the April 2004 *American Journal of Economics and Sociology*, pp. 275-90.

Money, Credit and Crisis

The amount of money

There is about $1.37 trillion of checking deposits and currency in circulation, 2006. Deposits and currency constitute "M1," which designates the total of fully-liquid money in the economy That amount is about 14% of the GNP.

Of course, money is an entirely fluid phenomenon. The static quantity, "M1," is only part of the story; the other part of the supply of spendable money is how quickly each recipient respends it, or in other words, money's velocity. The ratio of GNP/M1 is what standard macroeconomics texts call "velocity."*

How liquidity is created

How can anyone or any bank create net liquidity? A's asset is always B's debt on its flip side. Banks do create net liquidity, however, in spite of the flip side; that's what banks get paid for. The flip side makes it tricky and hazardous, which puts thrills and chills in the Magic Mountain of banking. People have been doing it, nonetheless, for centuries. Bank liabilities are more liquid than bank assets;

---

* More exactly it is "GNP-velocity." "Velocity" alone, in proper banking parlance, means transactions-velocity or deposit turnover. This is a much higher figure which covers the use of money in all intermediate transactions, not just those that enter into GNP.

that's what allows them to be loaned out as new demand deposits — which are spendable as fully-liquid cash.

Here's how they do it: the bank finds a borrower who will pledge some asset (collateral) to secure payment of a loan. It takes the borrower's IOU and records it on the asset side of its balance sheet. In return, it gives the borrower the bank's IOU, now called a demand deposit. (Originally it was a bank "note," a piece of paper reading "will pay to the bearer on demand...") This demand deposit goes on the liability side of the bank's balance sheet.

In the American colonial period, the original banks did not even accept deposits. They started, rather, by creating bank notes (like deposits, these are bank demand liabilities). There was little currency circulating for them to accept as deposits, so instead they created a currency by accepting collateral in return for issuing bank notes. When you cut through the fog, the effect is the same as though title to the collateral were now chopped into small units, circulating in bearer form.

Why does the borrower pay interest to the bank? The bank's IOU is worth more because it is liquid: the borrower can spend it immediately, and the bank must be able to cover, i.e. to redeem it. Banks borrow short, but lend long.

The bank's IOU is liquid because the bank spends money to make it so. That is how it uses the interest it receives from borrowers. Banks use their income to create liquidity by offering valuable services, such as guarding your money, paying cash on demand from an attractive building in a convenient location, clearing checks, holding reserves and maintaining a reputation for always meeting their obligations on demand. For those benefits, depositors are willing to forgo interest income.

Banks play the percentages, and are never literally in a position to perform on their contracts, that is, to redeem all their deposits on demand. Some have advocated "100% reserve banking," to avoid that. This cause is a remote dream and a diversion from reality. Required reserves provide an element of liquidity that is only specious. They are in dead storage and can never be used. So why are they required? Ceremony, symbolism, tradition and mystery. They are thought to help sustain confidence. The perceived need for such mumbo-jumbo reveals the basic instability of banking.

The workable alternative is to require banks to stay highly liquid by restricting their loans to commercial paper secured by highly liquid collateral, such as accounts receivable. Such short-term loans finance the working capital of businesses and are therefore automatically self-liquidating in a few months. The idea that liquidity is important is known as the "commercial loan theory," *aka* the "real bills doctrine." In England, it is called the "banking school" position. An early and eloquent advocate was Adam Smith, in *Wealth of Nations*.

Banks and their economist-spokesmen resist this policy, which they parody and flay mercilessly with all the considerable influence and authority at their command. Ordinary texts today foolishly dismiss it, citing the studies of Lloyd Mints, the predecessor of Milton Friedman at Chicago. Adam Smith, the apostle of *laissez faire*, is too regulation-minded for them. Chicago orthodoxy, now articulated by Milton Friedman, brooks no twilight shadow of qualitative control on bank lending.

The valid idea in "real bills" — not to be confused with "real estate" — is that banks should avoid lending on real estate collateral and for long terms. Default on real estate loans was the major cause of bank failures from 1929-33, the period in which half the nation's banks failed. Chicago orthodoxy has taken that disastrous cataclysm and stuffed it down the memory tubes. The resulting collective amnesia is one of the greatest, most brazen feats of thought control in history.

Why Chicago orthodoxy cannot tolerate the real bills doctrine

1. It implies there is some systemic weakness in the market, out of which collapses are generated. Chicago ideology demands that collapses be caused only by errors of short-term policy judgment by the Federal Reserve Board. It cannot accept the reality of factors outside the banking system — namely, the land-value boom and bust cycle.

2. It implies that banks need to be monitored more closely and specifically than they like to be. Chicago accepts general "quantitative" controls, and rather tight ones at that, in order to be rid of all specific "qualitative" controls. This ideology led directly to the Savings and Loan fiasco, as well as the Great Crash of 2008.

3. It withdraws a major support from the value of real estate, an interest with which Chicago identifies. It also tends to desanctify property as a good in itself, property for the sake of property. Rather, it points up the danger of using land as a "store of value" instead of using it simply as a factor of production.

Nevertheless, banks have followed Chicago and flouted the real bills doctrine once again, as they did in the early 1980s — and once again they are stuck with non-performing (defaulted) long-term loans backed by real estate collateral. In a larger sense, most corporate debt is secured by pledging corporate real assets, in every industry.

Why is bank regulation justifiable? Adam Smith never questioned it, because there are things that individuals can do one at a time which they cannot do collectively — and one of those things is liquidating real estate investments. Real bills as a policy compels the banks to stick with "self-liquidating" loans which turn into money through sale of the collateral to consumers. That is something that can be done collectively, because it is done routinely, daily, in the normal course of production and exchange.

Land, in sharpest contrast, is not self-liquidating. The cash flow from unappreciating land is just enough to pay interest on its purchase price. But most land today is appreciating. Its cash flow is less than enough, and must be augmented each year by additional outside payments. If we stop to remember that some 70% of all loans currently finance the purchase of real estate, we can see the outrageous load that collateralization of land values places on the financial system.

Land values, interest rates and investment

There is direct conflict between high land values and the rate of return on productive, job-making real investments. High land values may mean low rates of return on new investments. The high land values are supported by siphoning off part of cash flow to income payments to those who own the land, or to those who lend entrepreneurs funds to buy it. The combination of high credit-worthiness with low returns on newly-created capital can only spell trouble: banks expand as real investment falls. At the same time, rising land values discourage saving and encourage consumption, e.g. by using home-equity loans.

When land is so overpriced as to cut deeply into rates of return on job-making new investment, banks turn to taking land itself as collateral. When land gets so overpriced the borrowers can't pay the loans, banks panic, freeze up, and stop originating new loans. Then as old debts are paid, the money goes into the bank and never comes out again. What banks have created they can destroy. Just as expanding banks issue new money, contracting banks swallow it up again.

This is a major source of the notions of oversaving and cash-hoarding, notions so common in depressions. "Where has all the money gone?" people ask, and look under the mattresses of misers. Most of it has simply been retired by banks that collect old debts without originating new ones. The financial system is most vulnerable to collapse when an unexpected sharp rise of interest rates pulls the plug on the expected cash flows from durable capital, and from land. Land values are especially sensitive to interest rates; and doubly so in a rising market. Remember: banks borrow short, but lend long. If land value is the basis for a loan being repayable, and land value declines as interest rates increase, then we can see how shaky land values are as a basis for loans.

A bank that lends long gets repaid only slowly, and can therefore originate only a small volume of new loans each year, relative to its assets. A bank whose borrowers default is in the same pickle, only worse. And their pickle becomes everyone's pickle to the extent that we depend on them to finance the flow of investment that keeps The Great Wheel of economic life turning.

We will not undergo another banking collapse as extreme as Herbert Hoover's, because bank assets now include a higher fraction of Federal debt. This is undefaultable because the Federal Reserve System now stands ready — entirely too ready — to bail out the system by issuing new money. Default will therefore take the form of more and faster inflation, on top of the chronic slow inflation we have lived with for generations. Washington has fooled us into ignoring slow inflation by jiggering the Consumer Price Index downwards, e.g. by omitting housing and energy prices. It cannot paper over fast inflation so easily, and voter reaction may rise in a tsunami. Reforms will result. Let us hope they are better informed than the ones that gave us the system in place today.

Adapted from lecture notes for a college course of the same name. An expanded version of this essay appeared in After the Crash: How to Design a Depresssion-Free Economy, *2009, Wiley-Blackwell.*

Denying Inflation: Who, Why, and How

Henry George foreboded that landowners might take a growing wedge of the national "pie," or product. Labor's wedge might grow absolutely, as the whole pie grows, but still fall as a fraction.

It might even shrivel. In our times, George's grimmer scenario is coming true. Since about 1975, labor's wedge of the pie is shrinking as an absolute. "Real" wage rates have been falling since then. "Family wage" used to mean a breadwinner's wage high enough to support a family; now it means the combined wages of two adults. Many of these are "DINKS" (Double Income, No Kids) because that is all they can afford without cutting their customary material and educational standards.

The "real" wage rate is a ratio: the nominal money wage rate, divided by an index to the Cost of Living (COL). The higher the COL, the lower the real wage. Landowners cut into labor's share from both the top and the bottom, because the COL includes many products of land (like building materials and energy) and land itself (like homesites). Shelter costs are by far the largest part of household budgets.

The standard index to the COL is the Consumer Price Index (CPI), calculated and published regularly by the Bureau of Labor

Statistics (BLS). This index is, we will see, a political football.

Henry George said little about inflation because it was not a threat in his day. That was a time of "hard money" and the gold standard. Prices were stable or falling; *de*flation was the great bugbear. Today, though, to check on George's forecast, we have to distinguish between nominal money wages and real wages.

An old folk song offered the following wisdom about survival in the Everglades: "If the skeeters don't gyitcha then the gators will." If the skeeters of life are nicks taken from money wages, the big gator is the price of buying and owning a home.

Why deny inflation? Those in power have several reasons to understate rises in the cost of living (COL), measured by the CPI.

☞ *To mask the fall of real wage rates.* This is supposed to placate working voters. It is supposed to support orators declaiming that our standard of living is ever-rising, and we should all feel good. Actually, real wage rates have fallen steadily since peaking in about 1975. That is using the official Consumer Price Index (CPI) to measure rises in the COL. If the CPI understates rises in the COL, real wage rates have fallen even faster than the data show. As a by-product, this denial of inflation supports those who like to dismiss Henry George as a false prophet of doom.

☞ *To mask the fall of real interest rates,* making savers and lenders feel better, and more willing to lend to governments. In this age of massive and growing federal debts, the US Treasury depends on willing lenders more and more, to stay solvent.

☞ *To cut the real value of social security payments.* This point is straightforward. These payments are also indexed to the CPI. If the CPI understates the COL, real Social Security benefits fall every year. Congress gets to spend the savings on wastes like Alaska's "bridge to nowhere," redundant imperialistic ventures, tax cuts for major campaign contributors, and no-bid contracts for the well-connected.

☞ *To cut rises in labor union and other wage contracts* that are indexed to the CPI. The Federal minimum wage, like most state minima, is also indexed to the CPI.

☞ *To give the Federal Reserve Bank credit for having "tamed inflation,"* when in fact inflation of land prices is running wild.

A lesser point today, but important before Congress leveled out the rise of tax rates with income, is to slow the rise of income tax brackets, which are indexed to the CPI. Congress, briefly in a reasonable mood, enacted this sensible provision when enough people became aware that they were victims of "bracket creep." Bracket creep is when inflation boosts your money income into a higher tax bracket, although your real income has not risen.

However, if the true COL rises by 10%, while the CPI rises by only 5%, this provision no longer protects us against bracket creep. It just gives a talking point to those who claim to protect us. Sneaky! That is why you, dear reader, may have had a hard time following the bean under one of the three shells. Politicians are good at withdrawing promises. The sneakier the method, the easier it is for them to cover their tracks.

That is the "Why" of veiling inflation. Now let us look at the "How." There have been two major steps in recent decades.

First there was removing the costs of buying and owning homes from the CPI. The Bureau of Labor Statistics (BLS), the agency that calculates the CPI, did this from 1983 onwards. They didn't remove it altogether; that would have been too transparent. Instead they substituted the "rental equivalent" of housing. This is supposed to be what your house would rent for, or what you would pay to rent a similar house. It is a hypothetical and casual figure — sloppy and unverifiable, in other words — based simply on questionnaires to a sample of homeowners. It takes no account of the fact that some people *will,* and therefore everyone *must,* pay a premium to own, because of expected higher future rents and resale values.

The "rationale" (cover story) for doing this is that a home is both an investment and a residence, and only the residence cost belongs in the cost of living. In fact, the annual economic cost of owning a home is the market value times the interest rate (plus the property tax rate, homeowners' insurance, depreciation, etc.). When prices are rising we may deduct annual gain from the cost, but when prices are falling we then must add the annual loss to the cost of ownership, and now that losses are becoming current, there is no thought of adjusting the CPI for that. If the BLS were constructing a true measure of the COL they would be on top of this point; but they do not balance their act. They seize on reasons to lower the CPI, not to raise it.

Thus the land booms of 1983-89 and 2001-07 were mostly blanked out of the official published CPI of those years. The CPI rose gently as though the land boom never happened. In 2004 housing prices rose by 13%, while these "rental equivalents" rose only by 2%.

The CPI also takes no account of the price of extra land around some houses. It takes inadequate account of recreational lands, which now have displaced farming and forestry over whole counties and regions.*

The second major step was the Boskin Commission Report of 1995 (Newt Gingrich was dominating Congress), and its acceptance and implementation. Michael Boskin of the Hoover Institution was called upon to legitimize allegations that the CPI overstated

---

* And can we believe that the price of access to recreational lands has advanced as slowly as other prices? In 1946 a summer family membership in the Dorset Field Club, Vermont, cost $100, giving access to the links, tennis courts, and clubhouse privileges for three months. Today there is no access for non-members. A membership costs about $30,000, by private negotiation, and annual dues were $3,000 in 2003. Meantime, in the big leagues, Donald Trump is asking $300,000 or so for a membership in Ocean Trails C.C.; and even Rupert Murdoch is complaining about the greens fees at Pebble Beach, $450 for one round. I am grateful that I got my fill of golf when I was young and dad could afford it.

inflation. He and his Commission obliged, and supplied the rationale for several rounds of trimming down the CPI even more.

The Boskin Commission's advanced methodology included a lot of old-fashioned cherry-picking. They accumulated evidence supporting the foregone conclusion, and omitted contrary evidence. Most tellingly, they were silent about the biggest factor by which the CPI understates inflation: that is the use of "rental equivalence" in place of home prices. Now, shelter costs are about 40% of consumer budgets, and hence of the true cost of living. To accept an extreme understatement of shelter costs, while distracting us with lesser factors and arcane methodology, shows bias.

Most professional economists, sad to say, treat Boskin's report as holy writ. They come on like preachers, salesmen, or just cheerleaders, not like scientists exercising independent judgment. I have recently surveyed 20 current texts in Macroeconomics. They all list the same four "biases," in the same order, that they allege make the CPI overstate inflation. These are:

☞ *Substitution bias.* When the price of something rises, you use less of it, so it should be weighted less in the index.

☞ *Quality improvement bias.* Products of the same name keep getting better, so they say.

☞ *New product bias.* The CPI lags in showing how new gadgets raise our welfare. Microchip products, of course, are the example of choice.

☞ *"Discount bias."* The CPI scriveners assume that products sold in discount stores are of lower quality, when they really are just as good, according to Boskin et al.

As to the first point above: when the price of food rises, elderly pensioners turn to cat food. Now the cost of fresh fruits and veggies counts for less in their cost of living. They have shown a preference for cat food, whose weight in the CPI should rise, and they are as well off as ever. Hmmm — something fishy there.

Let's examine the second point above, quality improvement

bias. The texts give some examples, but not a single counter-example. Here are a few of the latter.

☞ Two-by-four dimensional lumber is no longer 2x4, but 15-20% smaller in cross-section, and of lower grade stock.

☞ Salmon is no longer wild, but farm raised in unsanitary conditions, and dyed pink (ugh).

☞ "Wooden" furniture is now mostly particle-board; "wooden" doors are now mostly hollow.

☞ New houses have remote locations, far from desired destinations.

☞ Ice cream is now filled out with seaweed products.

☞ Airline travel is no longer a delight but a series of insults and abuses.

☞ Gasoline used to come with free services: pumping the gas, checking tire pressure and supplying free air, checking oil and water, cleaning glass, free maps, rest rooms (often clean), mechanic on duty, friendly attitudes and travel directions. They served you before you paid. Stations were easy to find, to enter and exit. Competing firms wanted your business: now most of them have merged.

☞ Cold fresh milk was delivered to your door.

☞ Clerks in grocery and other stores brought your orders to the counter; now, many clerks, if you can find one, can hardly direct you to the right aisle.

☞ Men's suits came with two pairs of pants and a vest, and they fitted the cuffs free. Waists came in half-sizes.

☞ Socks came in a full range of sizes; shoes came in a full range of widths; the clerk patiently fitted the fussiest of customers.

☞ Public telephones were everywhere, not just in airport lobbies. Information was free; live operators would often give you street addresses.

☞ Public transit was frequent, and served many routes now abandoned.

☞ Autos used to buy "freedom of the road"; now they buy long commutes at low speeds and rage-inducing delays. One must now travel farther and buck more traffic to reach the same number of destinations. Boskin *et al.* dwell on higher performance of cars, and the bells and whistles, but rule out taking note of the cost-push of urban sprawl.

☞ Classes keep getting larger, with less access to teachers and top professors, and more use of mind-numbing "scantron" testing.

☞ Before World War II, an Ivy-league college student lodged in a roomy dorm with maid service and dined in a student union with table service, and a nutritionist planning healthy meals. All that, plus tuition and incidentals, cost under $1,000 a year (or, about $14.5K in CPI-adjusted 2007 dollars). Now, to maintain your child's place and status in the rat race, you'd put out $40,000 a year for a claustrophobic dorm and junk food. On top of that, a B.A. no longer has the former value and cachet. Now you need time in graduate and professional schools to achieve the same status. Many students emerge with huge student loan balances to pay off over life, with compound interest.

☞ Warranties on major appliances cost extra, aren't promptly honored, and expire too soon. Repair services and fix-it shops used to abound to maintain smaller appliances. Now, most of them are throwaway.

☞ Replacement parts for autos are hard to find, exploitatively overpriced, and are often ersatz or recycled aftermarket parts.

☞ Musical instruments are mass-produced and tinny instead of hand-crafted and signed.

☞ Many new "wonder drugs," if you can afford them, have bad side-effects, while old aspirin still gets the highest marks.

☞ A rising array of taxes and other payroll deductions stand between one's nominal income and what it might buy. Income and social security taxes are not counted as part of the CPI.

☞ Medical doctors once made house calls, in the dim mists of history. Since then, access has become progressively more difficult, until today... well you know, you've been there. In many small towns there is no doctor at all.

☞ In 1998 the BLS dropped auto finance charges from the CPI. And certainly the largest cost of consumer credit, mortgage interest, has been removed by use of the "rental equivalent" substitute, with never a squawk from Boskin.

☞ In 1995 the BLS eliminated an "upward drift" in the "rental equivalent" index, with no explanation. It is probably relevant that Congressman Newt Gingrich was in the saddle.

One could go on. Boskin *et al.* seem not to have considered counterexamples to their foregone conclusions. The BLS, succumbing to political pressure, keeps modifying the CPI to show less inflation, even while our daily experiences and shrinking savings tell us there is more. A 1999 study of the changes in the 20 years between 1978 and 1998 showed the cumulative effect of many changes had been to lower the CPI substantially *(Monthly Labor Review,* 6/99).

George warned that landowners might take most of the fruits of progress, leaving labor barely enough to survive. Critics have urged us, instead, to don rose-colored glasses. The rosiest of these is the CPI as manipulated to screen out bad news, especially news about soaring land prices. Let us be aware of who is manipulating the news, why, and how.

— Groundswell, *December 2005*

The Great Crash of 2008

———>◦<———

Galloping settlement sprawl, such as that of the last 16 years, has set us up for The Great Crash of 2008. It has the signs of being a Category 5.

There are two main varieties: urban sprawl, and continental sprawl. Let's start with a modest case of urban sprawl.

In Milwaukee County, Wisconsin, there are 17 municipalities. Only two of these are fully built-out: Shorewood and Whitefish Bay, north of the City along the lake. Each houses about 10,000 people per square mile in the green comfort of detached houses on tree-lined streets. The others are full of vacant and derelict land. The Central City itself has hollowed out badly, while also annexing the northwest corner of the County in 1960, still unfilled after 48 years.

At the density of these upper middle-class suburbs, the entire US population, 300 million, would require 30,000 square miles. That is the area of a circle whose radius is 98 miles. Or, if we divide the needed area among 50 states, it is the area of 50 circles of radius 13.8 miles each. Either way you cut it, or any other way, it is lost in the vastness of the USA.

Yet, while the City of Milwaukee hollows out, and the inner suburbs remain unfinished, Milwaukeeans spread into the neighboring counties, where growth is faster: Ozaukee to the north, Washington to the northwest, Waukesha to the west, and Racine to the south. In addition, some substantial fraction of factory jobs, during times of peak need, go to residents of small outlying towns or farms far away, who move in temporarily when opportunity knocks.

Milwaukee is not growing dynamically, so its sprawl is modest. For immodest, spread-eagle, classic American sprawl, look to new and upstart cities in much of Florida, Texas, Anchorage, Alaska, or Las Vegas, Nevada. Some older cities, however — like Albuquerque or Oklahoma City — manage to sprawl without being dynamic. In California, "From the redwood forests to the Gulf (of California)" urban sprawl inflates the price demanded for nearly every square foot of this land that "belongs to you and me" — or would, if we could afford it. As Woody Guthrie also sang, "Believe it or not you won't find it so hot if you ain't got that dough-re-mi".

Then there is continental sprawl. Old cities and regions stagnate or shrivel, while new ones balloon out of nowhere. Some once-leading cities, and their population ranks in 1890, are St. Louis, #4; Pittsburgh, #7; Buffalo, #9; Cincinnati, #11; Newark, #14; Jersey City, #15; Louisville, #17; and Rochester, #19. These shrinking cities are all in the quadrant northeast from St. Louis, fairly close together, along with surviving but diminished giants like New York, Boston, Philadelphia, Chicago, Detroit, Cleveland, Baltimore, and a dozen middling cities and most of the US. population, as of 1890. People and goods could get from one place to another within fairly short distances, by rail.

Some new big cities today that were not even on the radar screen in 1890 are Los Angeles, Houston, Dallas, San Diego, Phoenix, San Antonio, Honolulu, San Jose, Seattle, Portland, Atlanta, Miami, Charlotte, Las Vegas, Salt Lake, and Jacksonville. These are all outside the northeast quadrant, as the US center of population moves steadily southwestward, from southeast Indiana in 1890 to south central Missouri in 2000. It's not just the center that counts, though: it's the dispersion. Populations south and west of the center are widely scattered.

Each of these new cities represents the transfer of an entire subset of the economy. Cities grow, as Jane Jacobs showed so brilliantly, by import substitution. They and their regions grow more and more self-sufficient as they add people. Repair shops evolve into parts makers, and they into assemblers and manufacturers, some with national and world markets.

At the same time, to tie us together we have the Interstate Highway System, and many state highway systems. Interchanges create hundreds of new commercial nodes. In the short run these may seem to bring urban values to old farmland; in the long run, and in the aggregate, they create an artificial abundance of urbanesque land, an overhang that presages the crash phase of the cycle. They also create an overhang of deferred maintenance and replacement, for highways must in effect be rebuilt every 30 years or so, but at higher prices for cement. Worst of all they create a permanent commitment to wasting energy. These contingent liabilities have been hidden during years of euphoria. Today, as gasoline prices soar and tax revenues falter, they are all too visible. Too much land accessed, and rising costs of accessing it, combine to lower land prices.

We also have our inflated air transport system. The US has 15,000 civilian airports, more by far than any other nation or group of nations. The vastest of these, Denver International, takes 34,000 acres, or 53 square miles. Other oversized ports are mostly in the south and west: Dallas, Orlando, Kansas City, Atlanta, LAX, Seatac, and Miami, for example. Some eastern ports are much smaller: Washington National is 1,000 acres; busy LaGuardia is only 600. Many general aviation ports are smaller yet, down to under 100 acres. Estimating the mean civilian airport area at 400 acres, (military airports, not included here, average much bigger), 15,000 airports would require six million acres, or 9,400 square miles — about the area of New Hampshire.

While surface area is only one of the resources that air travel consumes, it is symptomatic of the daunting resource requirements of spreading people from Nome to Key West, from Eastport to Kauai, throwing in American Samoa and Puerto Rico and The

Virgin Islands, protecting them all with military airports and bases and their logistics, and linking them as tightly as Baltimore and Philadelphia. The soaring costs, led now by jet fuel, and security aggravations, and falling comforts of air travel, are beginning to drive home these rising demands on limited resources. Meantime, though, this nationwide transportation network has brought vast new areas inside the urban ambit. A rich Montana rancher and his wife can wing it into Denver or Vegas in their private plane for a night on the town; but how long can this dream of city-country affluence last?

To highways and airlanes let us add the power grid; huge interregional water transfers and systems; several new kinds of radio communication grids in bewildering novelty and abundance; the postal service grid; UPS and FEDEX grids; natural gas lines; the telephone grid; the banking network; the list goes on, and on. Most of these bring service not just to the end-points, but to most of the included interstitial lands.

How can land rents and values fall from oversupply, when land supply is fixed? This fixity feeds the delusion that land rents and values can only rise with population and capital formation. However, people and capital can spread out to encompass and fructify more land. That is sprawl, urban and continental (worldwide, too — but that's not covered here).

Professor Robert Murray Haig theorized in 1926 that if transportation costs fell to zero, there would be no urban land values: one location would be as good as another. That can't happen, of course, but lower transportation costs, as by an abundance of Ford's Model T's, would lower land rents and values. He presented this just as a cautious academic speculation, but did he see something coming? Seen or not, it did come right after he published.

To Henry George, "land speculation" meant holding land off the market waiting for a rise. He likened it to an unconscious "combination" (a cartel) of landowners creating an artificial scarcity. George missed the next trick, however. He attributed industrial depressions to inexorably rising rents and land prices that progressively squeezed labor and investors off the land and into the unemployment lines. It was too simple. A good explanation must account for land value collapses, like today's, playing a key role in the crash.

Like all cartels, the unconscious combination of land speculators creates a price umbrella under which new resources enter the market. This "price-umbrella syndrome" periodically creates an artificial surplus of land. At the same time, the lavish use of durable capital to bring settlers to all this new land creates a shortage of liquid capital, a shortage of loanable and investable funds, a rise of interest rates and a tightening of credit.

Austrian cycle theorists have dwelt on this tilting of what they call "the structure of production", with too much capital getting sunk irrecoverably in what they call "higher order" goods. Well and good, they are onto something big and vital. Unfortunately, though, they find its cause solely in "forced saving" from bank expansion, with no reference at all to its "geo-economic" roots, and the role of inflated land collateral enabling bank expansion. Worst of all, they see no remedy except forcing down wage rates.

Forces of containment, notably including George's land speculation, have imposed uneconomic scatter and sprawl on settlement. They have held back the logical areas for continuous settlement and forced the pioneers to move around and beyond them. If you examine a map of population density in the United States at any time in history, you see that urban scatter and sprawl have their counterparts in national patterns of land use, and they always have had, in spite of the "Indian menace."*

By 1890 the Census gave up trying to draw a "frontier line". The Director wrote, "the unsettled area has been so broken into by isolated bodies of settlement that there can hardly be said to be a frontier line"—a passage that Frederick J. Turner misread, I think, as he launched from it into his classic "Frontier in American History."

---

* A series of such maps to 1865 is in John D. Hicks, *The Federal Union*.

It was not the frontier that was passing, but the last vestige of orderly advance into it. The center of population continued to march west-south-westward, as settlements grew ever more scattered. In 1893 another boom ended, evoking the populist plaint, "In God we trusted; in Kansas we busted."

George himself did not, to my knowledge, call the crash of 1893, or explain its causes to his readers. It might have enhanced his reputation among later economists, and justified the subtitle of *Progress and Poverty*. By 1893, however, he was preoccupied with other issues, sick, and four years from death. Perhaps, also, he perceived that the facts did not exactly fit the simple scenario sketched in *Progress and Poverty*, and he lacked time to revise his model, in which by then he was heavily invested.

Georgists of the 1920's did poorly calling the real estate slump that began in 1926, and the stock market crash of 1929. As late as 1932, at the very nadir of The Great Depression, Harry Gunnison Brown, leading Georgist economist of the times, dismissed the wreckage around him as "a period of slack business" (*The Economic Basis of Tax Reform*). Albert J. Nock and Frank Chodorov preoccupied themselves with carping at Keynes and labor unions, preaching free markets as though they had discovered them — and as though the system had not crashed after 1929. They opposed all totalitarians in principle, but aimed most of their shots at FDR and The Allies, alienating a generation of earnest activist reformers.

Career-minded professionals have to pause before issuing pessimistic forecasts about land and securities markets, where confidence hangs by a thread. Senator Charles Schumer warned of the IndyMac Bank collapse, and critics immediately jumped on him for causing it. Homer Hoyt could publish his masterpiece in the deepest trough of depression, when anyone with eyes or ears knew the system had crashed, and revolution was in the air. Twenty years later Hoyt had gone into real estate consulting and land speculation, and declined to see any revival of his own cycle. Many have put down even Robert Shiller for puncturing the euphoria: Michael

Mandel, Chief Economics Editor of *Business Week*, recently published *Rational Exuberance*, whose title telegraphs its message, while the views of his sunny senior columnist Jim Cooper remain reliably upbeat, week after week, as we sink deeper into the mire. No one will fault Mandel or Cooper for pricking the bubble of "confidence."

I do not know of a single Nobel Laureate in Economics who forecast the present crash, or any other. Two of them, Chicago-Schoolers Robert Merton and Myron Scholes, founded Long Term Capital Management to demonstrate the brilliance of their investment theories. It went down in flames in 1997, saved only by a Federal bailout. Nothing daunted, media and public speakers seeking confirmation lean hard on citations of Nobel Laureates. The media might better consider others with better track records.

Modern Georgists enter this period of danger and opportunity in relatively good shape. Several have outstanding scorecards calling the current crash. These include Fred Foldvary (2007, *The Depression of 2008)*; Fred Harrison (2005, *Boom/Bust*); Michael Hudson (2007, "The New Road to Serfdom," *Harper's*); and Bryan Kavanagh (2007, *Unlocking the Riches of Oz*). Each has a slightly different take on it, but they all saw it coming and stuck their necks out to forecast it in print. One of their distinctive commonalities is their recognizing that land rent and values are many times higher than most economists realize, and so play a major role in macro-economic ups and downs.

These Georgists who foretold this crash deserve a hearing, in preference to those who failed, and certainly to those who still deny it. What solutions would they offer? I do not speak for them, and they are not of one mind, but the following elements seem reasonable and likely.

One, of course, is to raise more public revenue from taxes on property in general and land in particular. These include property taxes, of course, but in addition a host of other kinds of revenues. [*]

---

[*] See pp. 61-88.

One of them, which Michael Hudson has explained in several articles, is to reform the personal income tax to bear heavier on property income and lighter on wage income.

Another is always to base land assessments on current market value, and update them annually. 'Expert' appraisals of land are based on sales of comparables, and upward price trends. These sales, in turn, were influenced by appraisers who based their opinions on earlier comparables and upward trends, and so on. This is because there is no cost of production to check excesses. Thus a herd mentality can take over, divorcing prices from reality: 'Irrational Exuberance.'

Why, then, would I ask public assessors to join the misguided herd? Because the public assessor is the one valuer whose overvaluation stops the herd. The Assessor by law is supposed to follow a bull market, not outguess it. When the "exuberance" appears in his wisdom to be "irrational," his job is still to go along, not judge. When private fee-appraisers go along they confirm and reinforce a boom, but when the tax Assessor goes along he douses a boom with cold water: higher taxes. It was the lack of such an automatic remedy that let the farmland boom of the 1970s soar so high above reality, then the urban bubble of the late 1980s, and now, of 2001-07.

The present income-tax treatment of "capital" gains, which nearly forces the elderly to cling to their lands until they die, should be changed to a tax on annual accrual of value, as proposed by our same Professor Haig in the 1920s. The "Unplumbed Potential" article explains practical ways of doing this.

Banks should be regulated away from lending on land collateral. Following the South Sea Bubble (ca. 1720) there was such a movement in England. The emergence of the industrial revolution, flawed as it was, suggests the results were not all bad. Logically there is a powerful reason to regulate banks of deposit. This is because they are always technically insolvent, never able to meet their short-term liabilities from their long-term assets. A related reform might be to make mortgage notes part of the property tax base.

It is tempting to note that public debt has often been a more stable asset for banks than mortgages. Ever since FDR, banks have avoided the total dependency on mortgage loans that led so many to fail from 1929-33. Should we then limit banks to holding public debt? The problem is, it only takes one wild administration to bankrupt a nation by making a virtue of spending more and taxing less, egged on by certain extremist schools of economic theory. Federal providence is no guarantee of public thrift, either. In the 1920's when Andrew Mellon ran a Federal surplus, local governments and improvement districts ran wild with debt. In the 1830's, when Andrew Jackson ran a surplus, it was state governments that went broke. There is no simple mechanical substitute for sober judgment based on theory, and history, and selfless public spirit.

Meantime, where is hope? Cleaning up the mess left from the last few manic years will cost sweat and tears and fortunes, whoever undertakes it. Lower rents and land prices will finally let us recover, but the process of getting from here to there entails a fall from illusion to reality, from high to low, that will agonize many. New administrations will prolong the agony by trying to defer it. They will bail out a few of the victims and many of the culprits by raising the national debt and inflating the currency to validate bad debts and sustain land values.

Hope lies in observing how many cities and nations have risen from disasters to new prosperity. John Stuart Mill stressed in his *Principles* (1848) "the great rapidity with which countries recover from a state of devastation; the disappearance, in a short time, of all traces of the mischiefs done by earthquakes, floods, hurricanes, and the ravages of war."

Born-again San Francisco, 1907-30, makes a case study in fast recovery after it was devastated in 1906. It had no State or Federal aids to speak of; no oil or gas royalties; no power to tax sales or incomes or payrolls; no lock on Sierra water to sell its neighbors, as now; no finished Panama Canal, as now; no regional monopoly; no semitropical climate; and little flat land. Its great bridges were unbuilt – it was more island than peninsula. It had eccentrics, drunken sailors, race riots, vice, vigilantism — and boatloads of illegal immigrants, whose records were lost in the fire. It had fog, the Sierra wall to the east, and the San Andreas Fault, which will never go away. Statewide, mining was fading; irrigation barely beginning. How did a City with so few assets raise funds to repair its broken infrastructure and rise from its ashes? It had only the local property tax, and much of this tax base was burned to the ground. The secret is that it taxed the ground itself, raising money while also kindling a new kind of fire under landowners: to get on with it, or get out of the way. Developments are interdependent, so each owner could improve his land in the knowledge that other owners were subject to the same pressures, so needed complements would arise in sync with his own investment.

In 1907 the City Committee on Assessment, Revenue, and Taxation reported that revenues were still adequate, because before the quake and fire razed the city, 75% of its real estate tax base was already land value. The coterminous County and School District used the same tax base. San Francisco and Henry George were more in tune than perhaps either one realized. They did not rely just on cheerleading; they had a substantive program that worked.

This firm tax base also sustained San Francisco's credit to finance the great burst of civic works that was to follow. People flocked there to open businesses, and find jobs and homes. The City bounced back so fast its population grew by 22%, 1900-10, in the very wake of its destruction; another 22%, 1910-20; and another 25%, 1920-30. It did this without expanding its land area, and while providing wide parks and public spaces. It even pulled back from the treacherous filled-in level lands that had given way in the quake. On its hills and dales it housed, and linked with mass transit, a denser population than any major city except the Manhattan Borough of New York. It is these people and their works that made San Francisco so livable, the cynosure of so many eyes, and the commercial, financial, cultural, tourism, and light manufacturing center of the Pacific coast.

The whole US can follow this model today, but on a grander scale and adapted to modern technology and values. Skeptics will wonder how we can take more taxes from rents when they are falling. Here is the key: the effect of untaxing trade, enterprise, work, and production is to raise and sustain land and resource rents as a tax base. This does not work through raising asking and holdout prices, but rather by raising bid prices, activating the market. Today we recognize a great variety of new ways these rents manifest themselves to be tapped for public revenues. We can seize these opportunities, old and new, and pull ourselves out of the funk left by the great crash of 2008.

— Groundswell, *July–August 2008. Published as a pamphlet along with "How to Thaw Credit, Now and Permanently" by the Robert Schalkenbach Foundation, 2009*

How to Thaw Credit,
Now and Forever

—————⊰◦⊱—————

Working capital is the bloodstream of economic life. It is physical capital, the fast-turning inventory of goods in process and finished goods that supplies materials to the worker, and feeds and clothes her family. Short term commercial loans and trade credit buy it, but the capital is "real" — a fact often forgotten in the paper and virtual worlds of high finance, whence come the highest inner circles of government.

The bloodstream metaphor harks back to François Quesnay, an 18th century French physician turned economist. Quesnay drew on William Harvey's (1578-1657) earlier discovery of how blood circulates. Adam Smith and other classical economists followed Quesnay, distinguishing "circulating capital" from "fixed capital," the kind that is stuck in the ground or otherwise lasts for many years. Today we call the bloodstream metaphor "macroeconomics," elaborated but not always improved from Quesnay's insights.

Today, society's economic blood is drained down, and what's left is slushy. We need to restore and thaw it, and get it circulating, right away — as well as over time. To understand how, let's see what drained it away in the first place.

Vampire 1: public debt

Each Federal deficit draws more blood from the private sector. Cumulative deficits add up to the national debt. Washingtonians used to joke about a hick Congressman whom the voters returned for several terms because he never voted against an appropriation or for a tax bill; but now the Republicans, once the reliable foes of public debt, have become its champions. The debt was $900 billion when Reagan took office in 1981. In 1984 Mondale/Ferraro campaigned to stop the bleeding, but voters chose the lure of lower taxes and higher spending. When Bush *père* left office in 1993 the debt was $4,000 billion, a number so high we started counting it in trillions. From 1993-2001 the pendulum swung back as President Clinton came to terms with the newly-thrifty Republican Congress. Equally important, he did not invade any other nations. Some military bases were actually closed, rare as that is; others were mothballed. Now, however, Bush *fils* and his supportive Congresses have run the debt up to $11, $12, $13 trillion or more, depending on who's counting.

How did Reagan and Bush persuade themselves to invert traditional Republican doctrine? There were two main gurus: Art Laffer, Jr., and Robert Barro.

Laffer drew his famous curve on Dick Cheney's cocktail napkin in 1974, and changed the course of history. Taxes, said Laffer, suppress incentives so much that Washington can actually lower tax rates and collect more money. He stressed how taxes "suppress" incentives to work and to invest. Others also stress how taxes twist incentives so people allocate resources less efficiently.

Anyone who has read Henry George will relate to how taxes suppress and twist incentives. Laffer, indeed, quoted George enthusiastically. Tragically, though, he only got half (actually less) of George's idea. Laffer never specified *what* or *which* taxes suppress and twist incentives. George thought they all did, save one: he thought that rent, in its various forms, was the only sensible thing to tax; he noted that down-taxing other tax bases would enhance land rents and values as a tax base.

The voters loved Laffer's message of lower tax rates *cum* higher public spending, and Reagan used it to help win his election. Within a few years, however, it was clear that Laffer's tax cuts actually lowered revenues, and he lost favor — although his ideas lingered on until just yesterday in the highest circles of the Bush Administration.

The other new guru was Professor Robert Barro, then of Rochester, now of Harvard. Dick Cheney tersely summed up Barro's message: "Deficits don't matter." Barro argued that deficits today mean higher taxes tomorrow. Present taxpayers and savers will save more today to prepare for that burden of tomorrow. This higher private saving offsets government's dissaving.

It was not just Barro. Iconic Milton Friedman, the very avatar of anti-Keynesianism, chimed in with "Why twin deficits are a blessing" (*WSJ*, Dec. 14, 1988). (The other deficit was our national import balance.) Friedman had risen to fame by refuting Keynes and giving us "monetarism." Once in favor, however, with Keynes reduced to a memory, Friedman turned around and endorsed a new rationale for deficit finance.

This Barro-Friedman rationale has a seductive element of truth, but a greater error. The primary effect of deficit finance is that government bonds, to their owners, are an asset, a "store of value." George and others labeled bonds as "fictitious capital" — they are nothing but a lien on future taxpayers, yet they swell their owners' portfolios just as though they were real social capital. Thus they satisfy people's needs for retirement funds, and other comforts and joys of holding wealth. For most people, the marginal satisfaction from holding additional wealth diminishes as they hold more. Economists call this "the wealth effect."

By substituting for real capital, bonds lower people's marginal incentive to save and invest. Barro recognized this wealth effect. His point was that it is offset by the negative wealth effect of the prospect of higher future taxes, so "Deficits don't matter."

It is true that some bonds do represent real social capital, as when public bodies spend the money wisely and honestly on useful objects and services of general value, like scientific research, replacing worn-out roads and bridges, air traffic control, education, and so on. Ideally, all bonds would. The apparent dissaving would be offset by investing in public and human capital, raising incomes and land values to fortify future tax bases to retire the bonds.

History cries out, however, that nations in thrall to imperial overreach and its parasitic lobbies fritter away too much capital on warfare. Urban history shows how cities, counties, states, and nations fritter away capital by subsidizing urban sprawl.

Our huge and ongoing foreign trade deficit shows that the investment crowded out of domestic industry must exceed private sector gains from public spending. How could it be otherwise — when so much public spending goes to maintain hundreds of military bases around the world, bribes to manipulate foreign rulers, long wars without apparent net benefit to the US, and the whole military-industrial complex?

An analogy to slavery may make this clearer. It is a truism of economic history that slaves in the Old South satisfied their owners' need for wealth, substituted for real capital in their portfolios, and led to a culture of extravagance. Formation of real capital suffered. So did the slaves — who also substituted directly for farm capital. Underequipped Confederate soldiers paid the price on the battlefield.

As a secondary effect, the prospect of future taxes is a liability to bondholders and other future taxpayers — the "negative wealth effect," as Barro says. It is unlikely that this distant future possibility shows up on the liability side with the same weight as the bonds on the asset side, as Barro's critics have pointed out. Most of these critics, right as they are, have failed to add that our tax structures at every level have been growing more regressive. Future taxpayers are more and more likely to be the working poor.

The net marginal satisfaction from holding wealth actually diminishes more and faster when the wealth consists of real capital. This is because owners of real capital, especially working capital, must manage and maintain it, and constantly replace it as it turns over. This is hard work, and risky, too. Bonds, in contrast, keep in a vault with no such cares. Only the most durable investments — gold, land, and some common stocks — can compete with government bonds in this respect. So big savers, as their wealth accumulates, more and more turn away from supplying working capital like short term commercial loans and trade credit.

Working capital, the coursing bloodstream of our private economy, needs a heart — the owner-entrepreneur — to pump it through the system and recirculate it constantly, often several times a month. But the stoutest heart cannot pump blood that is not there.

Government bonds "crowding out" private wealth from portfolios is part of how government borrowing takes capital away from the private sector. The other part of crowding-out is dynamic. When the Treasury sells new public bonds they crowd out new private bonds and corporate IPOs and new investing in unincorporated businesses.

The Greater Dracula: land value

Notwithstanding all that: there is a Greater Dracula sucking blood from our economy. Land value is invisible to most economists. Those cited above, however deep their insights about public debt, rarely mention it; their neo-classical training blinds them to it.

We noted earlier that US bonds serve as "fictitious capital" to their owners, a store of private value that is not real social capital. So do land values, only much more so. They satisfy the need to hold assets without any corresponding net social saving. Individuals may save to buy land, but the seller dissaves in the same sale. Most home buyers, in fact, finance their purchase from selling a previous home. Mere ownership turnover of a fixed stock does not constitute net social saving.

Not only do land values substitute for real saving, they promote dissaving. Notoriously, we have just been through several years of homeowners' heeding the siren songs of bankers to "unlock the equity" in their land to pay for cruises, cosmetic surgery, golfing, yachts, vacation homes, fast cars, stables, you name it. Rising land values seem to the owners like current income that they can spend as they wish, so long as banks are ready to lend on them. That is the dynamic side of it. Then, after the values have risen, they stand in for wealth to some owner or lender — muting, via the wealth effect, their urge to save.

Unlike the case of US bonds, there is no corresponding "negative wealth effect" with rising land values. They rise spontaneously; they are a free gift from human fecundity and progress. They result from our having traveled a few more years through time. Land has simply grown more highly rentable, in the rosy visions of optimists, the ones who dominate the market. The land in a portfolio of assets is not, *per se,* a debt that someone must retire.

It is true that prospective buyers are now poorer, in that they must pay more for land. This might stimulate them to save more. However they, too, share the vision of higher future rents, so they are paying more simply because they think they are getting more. Sometimes they actually are. If the price-to-rent ratio rises it is because of the promise of higher future rents or resale values — whether or not the promise comes true.

What about common stock? I omit it here for three reasons. One, a good deal of its value represents indirect ownership of real estate. Two, in our times its total value has dropped well below that of dwellings. Three, the media and public consciousness greatly overstate its role in the economic scheme. News reporters parrot phrases like "a fall of stock prices has wiped out a trillion dollars of wealth." Most of the wealth is still there; in most cases all that's changed is expectations of future earnings, or taxes, or subsidies, or bail-outs, or even more trivial and superficial matters.

Housing and land values together

Ever since 1913 the capital invested in owner-occupied housing, and the land used for it, have enjoyed virtual exemption from the tax levied on other forms of income. Income? What income? If A rents a house to B for cash rent, that rent is taxable income. If A evicts B and moves into the house for his own use, the taxable cash flow stops. In either case, however, A receives a flow of imputed income from land value appreciation. Economists recognize it as income, but Congress does not tax it as such.

Imputed income of owner-occupied land is not taxed, but interest on mortgages is deductible, unlike other consumer interest (e.g. on credit cards and auto loans). Most small homeowners do not itemize, so the deductibility of interest (and property taxes, too) mainly benefits richer people. If you own six or seven houses, a horse farm, a duck blind, a ski chalet, a lakeside cottage, a wild forty for hunting or riding, a golf club membership, a beachfront, etc., all that imputed income is exempt too.

The net income of a house — the building *per se,* that is — is far less than its service flow. The owner must rewire, replumb, reroof, replace the furnace and air, pay the utilities, fight termites, remodel and redecorate — and still lose value by depreciation and obsolescence. The site of the house, however, demands none of those, and generally appreciates besides — not in 2009, obviously, but more years than not. The current crash should not blind us to what has happened since, say, 1970. A $35,000 dwelling bought then, through a chain of sales and purchases, was worth about $1,100,000 in 2006, and still after a steep drop is worth about $700,000.

Unearned increments (aka "capital gains") are not taxed until time of sale, if that ever comes, although owners may take out cash, tax free, any time, by using a line of credit or other form of mortgage, whose interest is deductible. If one does sell for a gain the tax is deferred so long as you buy another home of equal or greater value within a two-year window. Most homeowners continue this chain of deferral until death, at which time all the accrued gains are exempted forever — the so-called "Angel of Death" provision.

As to rental housing the renter cannot deduct the rent, but the owner's rents are generally untaxed because the owner can often tax-depreciate the building much faster than it really depreciates economically, wiping the rental income off his tax return. This same benefit also goes to office, commercial, and industrial buildings, but not to wage and salary incomes, all of which are taxed — even the part that is taken away as the social security tax, as well as social security pension payments.

When owner A has depreciated a building down to zero he sells to owner B, who does it all over again, and so do C, D, E, ... etc. until the building dies. When A sells to B the excess depreciation is nominally "recaptured" by taxing the nominal gain, but it is called a "capital gain," subject to a lower tax rate, at a later date, a higher price level, and a new tax structure lowered from when A took the original depreciation.

When B tax-depreciates the building, he normally depreciates a good deal of land value, too, even though the land is *appreciating*. Michael Hudson and Kris Feder (1997, Levy Institute) have shown how all this lowers the taxable income from all the income property in the USA to an aggregate of zero — Repeat, ZERO!

Little people get a cut of the action, too, enough to nail down their votes, but it's the big people who own several mansions apiece in the choicest locations. Ever since labor got the vote in the mid-19th Century, politicians have fostered *la petite propriété* as a bulwark to protect *la grande propriété* from the rabble.

The arrangement has been and is bipartisan. Call something "housing" and it becomes sacred, a fetish, unassailable, even if it has 82,000 attached acres and 17 miles of coastline. The result has been a massive overallocation of the nation's capital stock and land to housing. We are "overhoused America." There's not "too much housing" in an absolute sense; many folks at the bottom are underhoused. Thousands are homeless, including many children. That's a matter of unequal distribution, but also at the core of modern politics. The former rabble have become the rationale for exempting the playgrounds of the rich, and the little castles of the middle class, from taxation.

All that housing and land for the mansioneers take capital and land away from other uses, and sequester it in unrecoverable form. Housing pays out slowly at best, and a corresponding 30-year mortgage ties up the lender's capital in a highly visible and countable way. A bank can't make new loans much faster than it recovers capital from the old ones. So we reach a point, as now, where new loans are hard to come by — to meet payrolls, buy materials, and produce the daily needs of life.

That's "at best." At worst, builders glut the market, values drop, and the capital is not even recovered slowly, it's lost forever. Thus this housing capital is frozen. Its "net service flow" above expenses goes not to recover capital, but to pay interest. Then an oversupply gluts the market so the owner cannot sell without a big loss. Finally, bank loans secured by mortgages on this housing go bad, leading to a financial meltdown.

This is not just a domestic matter. Wall Street has been peddling these mortgages all over the world, and the international bills are coming due. We need to export more, but we can't export the surplus houses — and we can't recover the capital.

So what are Congress and Treasury and Ben Bernanke proposing along with the bailout? More of the same: raising the debt some more to save the housing-land market and the banks that have inflated it. Supply-siders, faced with crisis, convert quickly into demand-siders; free-market fanatics into *dirigistes*. Alan Greenspan himself has admitted to Congress that deregulation failed. Traditional Keynesian macro-economic thinking has risen again in the high places in Washington. The leading physicians picture clogged Wall Street as a case of cardiac arrest, to be cured by what FDR, in a more rural age, called "pump-priming."

Tragically, the 2008 Nobel Laureate, Paul Krugman, like other influential liberals, is reverting to the same old demand-side panaceas. "...right now, increased government spending is just what the doctor ordered, and concerns about the budget deficit should be put on hold" (*NY Times*, Oct. 16). This does not augur well.

Where is this new Federal money to come from? Borrowing from the public? That would mean more crowding-out of private borrowers, the very ones we need to have put capital back into the private sector. The other fallback is borrowing from Bernanke's willing Fed which will create new money, paper and virtual. New money without real goods behind it means inflation, more imports with fewer exports, devaluation, and a real risk that our foreign creditors will rebel.

Ben Bernanke has staked his reputation and our economy on his belief that we can depend indefinitely on a glut of savings in foreign lands. I suppose that comforting faith helped persuade him to accept his present job, but his claim seems dreamy and even arrogant now that the glory days of American hegemony are fading fast away. Wall Street has already sullied its credibility by dumping bad paper on the world. The US Treasury is not far behind. Let's ask what we should be doing instead.

Solutions

It's time to think big: it's survival time for the USA. We need to tap two enormous sources of capital that the vampires have created, one public and one private.

The government can create great gobs of lifeblood capital and quickly transfuse it into private arteries. We can do this without any giveaway, without rescuing failed banks with overpaid CEOs, without overpaying for toxic debt while pampered executives use our money to throw themselves lavish parties. We can do this without Federal meddling with free markets and enterprise and playing favorites with bailout billions.

The principle is simple: pay down the national debt. It's called "reverse crowding-out." Even as you and I, governments can save, by earning more and spending less. The question would arise, in what shall the government invest without interfering in private markets? Thanks to our past prodigality the answer is easy: invest in paying the debt. Turn the vampire into a source of fresh blood, bringing new life and vitality to the once-hale, now pale and failing private sector.

The principle may be easy but the practice is hard: we must tax more and spend less. However the present plan is to spend more anyway, selectively bailing out prodigals and debtors and the very culprits who led us into this morass. Better to invest in the nation's own credit, while pumping new capital back into the private sector. We have to do it soon anyway, and now is the time before interest eats us alive, our creditors lose faith and withdraw, the dollar collapses, and we become history's biggest fallen braggart, bully, pariah, and moral object lesson to illustrate *Proverbs* 16:18: "Pride goeth before destruction, and a haughty spirit before a fall."

But how, one naturally asks, can government tax more without suppressing and bleeding the very private economy we aim to revive? This leads us back to the second and Greater Dracula defined earlier: land value, what is really meant by "housing" when we read about the housing bubble: the part, in other words, of Henry George that Arthur Laffer suppressed.

Land value, we have seen, is fictitious capital, an asset and store of value for individuals, with no real social capital behind it. By taxing it and lowering its value we do not destroy any capital. On the contrary, we raise the owners' propensity to create real capital to restore the missing store of value. We also raise revenues without suppressing or twisting the incentives of free markets, as generations of economists have shown and agreed.

As for how, this writer has published a catalogue of no less than sixteen ways to tax land and resource values at every level of government, using income taxes and severance taxes and even certain kinds of user charges, along with the obvious and traditional property tax. For some examples, we can and should levy what Dick Netzer called "a family of user charges" for preempting space on, over, and under city streets. We should charge people, cities, water districts, power companies, and others for withdrawing water from surface and underground sources, and harnessing power drops. We should let each building be depreciated only once, by the original builder, and land never. We should rent out, rather than auction off, the radio spectrum, adjusting values quickly and often as the market rises. We should tax polluters, rather than paying them not to pollute. There is a great deal more; the taxable capacity of land is greater than many LVT advocates realize.

Retiring public debts is not enough. Andrew Jackson did it, 1829-37, and kicked off the greatest land boom and bust of the 19th Century. Andrew Mellon did it, as Secretary of the Treasury, 1921-32, and repeated the experience in the greatest debacle of the 20th Century. Where did they go wrong? It's of no benefit to pay off the national debt if the Greater Dracula, land speculation, guzzles away all the blood. In both decades land values swelled and working capital ran short. From 1798 to 1929 the 18-year cycle of land booms and crashes was broken only once, in 1911, 18 years after the crash of 1893. What went right then? That was the only time before or after when the nation's treasuries depended mainly on the property tax, and there was no big runup of land values.

The changes I propose are massive and radical, I know. People will resist, will object, will twist and turn and contort in dozens of ways, as Washington is now doing, to protect banks and landowners and the current power structure, resisting the unwelcome inevitable. They have eaten, drunk and been merry on low taxes, cheap credit, foreign loans and rising land values. Meet The Great Reckoning: it is time to foot the bill. We can do it and turn America healthy in one stroke by taxing land values and rents to retire public debts.

— Groundswell, *November–December 2008*

The writer owes Polly Cleveland for her searching criticism of an earlier draft. Remaining errors are, of course, my own. — M.G.

Turgot's Legacy:
Our Commerce Clause

⟫◇⟪

This is a story of the ideas of an 18th Century Frenchman, A.R. Jacques Turgot. His bones are buried, like all, yet the ideas were born again, and again. They always will be, because they illumine and solve universal and ongoing economic and human concerns.

Anne-Robert Jacques Turgot was an outstanding public servant, economic philosopher and social reformer in 18th Century France. He first made his mark as Royally-appointed *Intendant* of the *Limousin*, encompassing Limoges, 1761-74. An Intendant enjoyed considerable latitude and autonomy, although few chose to use it as aggressively and constructively as Turgot did, for that was hard work and might interfere with traditional graft and sensual amusements. Limousin was a district of poor soils; most tenants were sharecroppers *(metayers)*. Turgot observed the incentive structure closely, and later wrote on it concisely, anticipating by two centuries some findings of Gale Johnson and Steven Cheung.

Turgot was a friend of Vincent de Gournay, prominent capitalist entrepreneur and sometime *Intendant* of Commerce for all of France. Thus Turgot learned to appreciate commerce and industry, as well as agriculture. He was friendly with François Quesnay and his group called "Physiocrats", but scouted their cult-like tendencies and their overemphasis on agriculture and other extractive industries. Turgot saw that industry and trade were also productive, and devoted himself to encouraging them.

In Limousin he abolished the mandatory *corvée*, (roadwork in lieu of taxation). He improved roads by other means like taxing the lands they served. He was offered advancement to jurisdictions more favored by nature, but he conscientiously refused, in order to complete his reforms in Limousin. His Results were impressive. Kaolin was found near Limoges, and its ceramics (Haviland China) grew famous. It is plausible and likely that Turgot's economic reforms fostered the growth of this industry.[*]

In 1774 the new King Louis XVI made Turgot Comptroller-General for all France. Turgot set about removing interprovincial trade barriers, which he perceived as a major barrier to French prosperity. He coined the term *Laissez-faire (Laissez faire, laissez passer, le monde va de lui-même).*[†] He also set about reforming the tax system, subjecting the previously exempt lands of the first and second Estates[‡] to forms of property taxation. This was in the spirit of the age, the Age of Enlightenment (Science, Art and Letters, Philosophy), and Benevolent Despotism. It was appropriate for France, the most advanced and sophisticated nation of Europe, to lead the way.

These jolting changes set off alarm bells, however, among the leaders of the First and Second Estates. They epitomized their reaction in their notorious *Rémonstrance against the six edicts of Turgot* (1776), containing some of the most reactionary postulates imaginable, so as to seem today like a satire that a Swift or Voltaire might have forged to mock them. They enlisted the new Queen, Marie Antoinette,[§] to their cause. King Louis XVI was filled with good

---

[*] I have not sought nor stumbled on direct evidence or study of the matter, but trust that some scholar has done or will do so.

[†] "Let do and let pass; the world goes on of itself." There is a touch of Chinese Taoism in Turgot.

[‡] The Clergy and the Hereditary Aristocracy, respectively.

[§] Ironically, Marie's brother, Joseph II of Austria, embraced Turgot's reforms as enthusiastically as he did the music of Mozart, and would have led Austria into primacy in Europe had he not, like Mozart, died young.

intentions, but wilted under this pressure and replaced Turgot, first with Necker and then Calonne. These advanced token reforms but without the needed energy and conviction, for the Geocracy was strong, entrenched and self-righteous. Necker and Calonne thus simply paved the way to July 14, 1789. Turgot, meantime, retired to the country and died peacefully in 1781.

While Intendant of Limoges he published his *Reflexions sur la Formation et la Distribution des Richesses* (1766). This short, compact work contains much of the essential wisdom that Adam Smith soon was to popularize and expand with *The Wealth of Nations* (1776). Turgot stressed the important roles of capital, and free markets. He favored letting the market determine interest rates — not from dogma, but from observing the results of John Law's ruination of French banking in 1720. He favored combating poverty by relieving the poor of taxes, while raising revenues instead from taxes on the value of land – including lands traditionally exempt or undertaxed. Smith visited France in 1766 and consulted extensively with Turgot, a man whose practical turn of mind made him a congenial tutor for Smith.

Many of America's "Founding Fathers" visited France around the same time, and learned from Turgot, Quesnay, and the sect that gathered around Dr. Quesnay, who had been installed at Versailles as physician to Madame Pompadour, influential mistress to Louis XV. One could even consider this Frenchman to have himself been one of our Founding Fathers. The Commerce Clause of the US Constitution did for the new USA exactly what Turgot had tried to do for France: it guaranteed free trade among the states. For a long time it also prevented states from using excise taxes to raise revenue, forcing them back on the property tax, just as Turgot recommended for France. Some noted American visitors included Franklin, Jefferson, Paine, Madison, Monroe, Adams, and others. Growing American hostility to England meant growing friendship with France, and the American Revolution plus the ascendancy of Jefferson sealed a long Franco-American friendship and alliance.

It was also, of course, the Age of Reason, and the flowering of Enlightenment and Science. Turgot, like Quesnay, admired the work of William Harvey on the circulation of blood. Where Quesnay drew up his complex *Tableau Economique* (aka "*Les Zigzags*" by ladies of The Court) Turgot simply wrote that investing is "the beneficial and fruitful circulation that animates all the work of society, ..." — thus capturing the basic idea of modern macro-economics, in much simpler language than usually imposed on readers.

Smith's *Wealth of Nations,* a relaxing chatty read full of history and examples, eclipsed the skeletal language of Turgot; Turgot's *Reflexions* sank into relative obscurity. Smith, meantime, was forced to make Turgot's points in much less direct language, dependent as he was on his patron, the Duke of Bucchleuch, one of the biggest, if not *the* biggest, landowner in Great Britain. Smith also depended on the friendship of "Champagne Charlie" Townshend, author of the "Intolerable Acts" and other excises that Britain sought to impose on the American colonies.* By the time of our Revolution Turgot was dead and largely forgotten. Other Frenchmen like P.S. DuPont, Quesnay's disciple, and LaFayette, a non-intellectual romantic, Albert Gallatin, a transportation planner, Audubon, an ornithologist, and even Jean LaFitte, a pirate, gained more renown in America. Alexis de Toqueville, a patronizing French aristocrat whose writings flattered Americans' image of themselves, was very popular.

However the spirit of Turgot rose from the grave — call it *Tod und Verklarung* (Death and Transfiguration) — during the Progressive Era, in the work of Henry George, the American land reformer. Like Turgot, George favored raising revenues by taxing the vast lands of "The Robber Barons" in order to relieve workers and merchants from taxation. George even dedicated one of his

---

* These included a tax on tea imports, now revived in memory by the American Astroturf "Tea Party" movement. In fact, the original "Boston Tea Party" was more a protest against the monopoly of the British East India Company than against Townshend's minimal tax.

books, *Protection or Free Trade? (1886),* to Turgot, and founded a movement that helped lower American tariffs and raise American property taxes and put more stress on the land portion of real estate tax valuations.

The high point of Turgot's revival, however, came in 1917. The Great Red Scare succeeded in ending the Progressive Era in America. Since then property taxes have steadily fallen, step by step. Excise taxes, that Turgot hated so, have returned as state sales taxes, unknown before about 1931. A highly regressive payroll tax, equivalent to the old *corvée*, has become our largest Federal revenue source, swamping out the corporate income tax, the estate tax, and now even edging out the personal income tax, which is still at least slightly graduated nominally (but not really, if you allow for the 15% cap on capital gains and dividends, the total exemption of imputed property income, and the effective exclusion of most income from renting out real estate). America has become a Geocracy again, as much as France was under its *Ancien Régime.* That that may surprise many readers is a measure of how thoroughly property interests have captured and dominate modern media and higher education, too. If Turgot is to rise again, it will have to be the work of our generation and the next. Let us teach and work for a peaceful transition, as in The Progressive Era, unlike the French, Russian, Chinese, and other Revolutions when "ignorant armies clashed by night."

— Georgist Journal, *Summer 2012*

The Reburying
of Martin Faustmann

Faustmann was a German forester of mathematical bent. In 1849 he published a short tract with a long German title that we might freely translate as "When to cut a tree." Basically, his answer was: "When it stops growing fast enough to earn interest on its own embodied capital, plus rent on the land underneath it." He showed that this was the way to maximize the annual rent of the land, or *Bodenrente,* and the value of the land in perpetuity (*Bodenerwartungswerte),* through an infinite chain of cycles. He also showed this is the way to maximize the net value of a "going concern," or "normalized" forest, with ages staggered from one to maturity (a demonstration also found later in Wicksell*, who applied it to wines first, and then to whole economies).

Faustmann's Formula became a footnote in the forestry literature, where it was generally dismissed as being too mathematical, or too theoretical, or too abstract, or too severe, or too something, anything a forester could use to dismiss it. Professional foresters simply did not like it because it provided a way to show that the use of land

---

* Knut Wisksell (1851-1926) was a leading Swedish economist of his times, esteemed by both Austrian and Keynesian economists. His famous "grapejuice model" is in his *Lectures on Political Economy* (pp. 172-76 of the English translation by E. Classen, 1938).

in forestry could often not compete with other uses that yielded quicker and more frequent returns, not just in the short run but sustainably over time — infinite time.

Professional economists, wrestling myopically with the same problem, never consulted the forestry literature, and came up with a variety of wrong solutions. Some, like the US Forest Service, said "Aim for the 'culmination of mean annual increment' (CMAI), which maximizes the annual return to the land — if one can ignore interest costs." Others like Irving Fisher and R. G. D. Allen, said "Cut the tree when its growth rate falls below the rate of interest," — ignoring the cost of holding the land. Austrian economists like Menger, supposedly obsessed with their "period of production" as exemplified by timber, and surrounded by German foresters, never heard of Faustmann or his ideas.

The one economist to take heed was Bertil Ohlin, who derived the solution himself in 1921, but never consulted the forestry literature to discover Faustmann had scooped him by 70 years. Then, like Winston Churchill's man who stumbled across the truth, Ohlin got up and hurried on as though nothing had happened. Others, like Kenneth Boulding, advised maximizing the internal rate of return on the planting cost — a remarkably banker-like position for a man known as a green conservationist.

There were elegant variations on all these. Friedrich and Vera Smith Lutz said Faustmann's idea (they had another name for it) was right for individual trees, but wrong for normalized or staggered rotations. Some liked CMAI if you deduct planting costs; others refused to deduct planting costs. Some said that the cost of planting a replacement tree should be treated as part of logging costs, thus letting it be expensed for income tax purposes. Powerful Senators and Congressmen from timberland regions (a third of the United States is timberland) promoted formulae designed to maximize income-tax benefits for timberland owners, have timber declared to be a "capital asset" with a lower tax rate, and consider planting a current expense deductible from ordinary income. In state capitols, timber interests got timber exempted from property taxes, substituting yield taxes much too low to be revenue-neutral. In several states, standing timber itself is exempt from property taxes, while the land under it is separately assessed using formulas written by the industry, or its cat's-paws in Schools of Forestry, designed to minimize the tax valuation of the land.

The most valid criticisms of Faustmann came from ecologists and the like ("tree-huggers" to the loggers), because Faustmann (like Ronald Reagan later) put little or no value on scenic beauty ("if you've seen one redwood, you've seen 'em all"). Watershed protection is finally getting more recognition as a relevant value. Wildlife habitat is a value. To many people, virgin forests are a religious experience (loggers sneer at these as "Druids"). Forests are also beloved by hunters, whose alliance with "tree-huggers" and "Druids" is an ironic marriage of opposites.

In 1957 this writer took advantage of a Ford grant, arranged by my Chairman Addison Hickman*, to whom I am eternally grateful. I probed into the interesting question of "When to Cut a Tree?" I came up with what seemed to me a correct math solution, and prepared to claim it as my own. Prudentially, I first surveyed the forestry literature and discovered Faustmann had been ahead of me by about 108 years — but had been virtually ignored by foresters, and was totally unknown to economists.

To my delightful surprise, my little monograph, crudely mimeographed as an Ag Experiment Station Bulletin in North Carolina, made a hit. A few economists appreciated it for what I meant it to be, a macro-economic metaphor showing the benefits of faster capital turnover, using forest management simply as an easily expounded example. I slowly learned, though, that its popularity had a different cause, partly a product of the business cycle stage we then were then in. Many forest owners and their bankers were looking for new reasons to log faster, caring little or nothing for the causes I

---

* He chaired the Economics department at North Carolina State College (now the University of North Carolina - Raleigh).

was pushing (the welfare of society by speeding capital turnover to maximize employment). I had unwittingly played into their hands, giving them a new tool to forward their case. John Walker, CEO of Simpson Timber Company, was especially enthusiastic, and modestly came up with improvements on my exposition.

Next thing I knew, Bill Allen of UCLA, who had greeted my Faustmann idea so warmly in 1967, published a textbook falling back on the Fisher-Allen solution (that was R. G. D. Allen, not Bill) that I had refuted in 1957.* I never asked him why, and this is not the place to speculate. Paul Samuelson, who had written in support of my Faustmann solution, forgot all about it when upholding his end of the Cambridge Controversy, although it could have helped him refute the "Reswitching" model.† The sad fact is that Faustmann, after his *Tod und Verklärung*, was re-killed. Ideas may become chic when the stars are aligned, exploited for what good they might do special interests, then washed away with the trash — especially when they might be used to support raising taxes on land values or other property income.

This writer became *persona non grata* at Resources for the Future, Inc. , in 1972. I was not without fault, but a sea of troubles beset me when it became clear that I was extending my forestry research into forest taxation, and uncovering the shocking undertaxation of American forest holdings, both as property and as

---

* Allen, R. G. D., 1930. *Mathematical Analysis for Economists*, and Fisher, Irving,1930. *The Theory of Interest*. Fisher is the better-known of these two, and his authority is often cited — but they both left out land rent. Ironically, Fisher was the mentor of the Georgist economist Harry Gunnison Brown, whose horizons he limited.

† A long debate between economists from Cambridge University, led by Joan Robinson, and American economists led by Paul Samuelson of M.I.T. Since M.I.T. is in Cambridge, Massachusetts; it is now universally called "the Cambridge controversy." It had to do with the effect of interest rates on financial maturity of things like timber, i.e. "when to cut a tree," but by the time Samuelson got entangled in this he forgot all about his previous endorsement of Faustmann, and came off poorly.

income-yielding assets. I declined when a charming forest lobby-ist offered to wine, dine, and yacht-entertain me, but that was not enough. My then-employer, from that day to this, has listed some giant forest holders among its grantors. Problems overwhelmed me. A leading forest economist from Yale wrote threatening to attack me in scholarly journals if I published my findings. Marion Clawson, a friend and role model to me, used my mathematics to condemn forest managers in the National Forest Service and the Bureau of Land Management, with never a peep against private forest manag-ers. A Lincoln-Foundation grantee from Claremont Men's College attacked me on technical grounds in the *Western Economic Journal,* while the Editor of that Journal, whose office abutted his, refused to publish my reply.

Even more overt have been the recent experiences of Governor Bob Riley of Alabama, and Professor Susan Pace Hamill of the University of Alabama School of Law. Hamill is an activ-ist Christian who also teaches tax law, and became conscientiously aware of how Alabama's highly regressive tax system violates biblical principles of social justice. Alabama is highly churched, so she and Riley joined forces to bring its tax system into line with churchly doctrines. They began with its forest lands, which are vast, and virtu-ally untaxed. Many churches supported a Riley-Hamill Initiative, but many others, with the most money and influence, disappointed them, campaigning actively against and defeating their initiative.

New Hampshire State Legislator Richard Noyes, represent-ing North Salem, was a conservative Republican who even sup-ported the efforts of George H. W. Bush to sunset the capital gains tax, a cause dear to timber owners but not to me. At the state level, however, he pushed for a statewide tax on land values, consistent with his belief in making state governments work better. He did not target timberlands *per se,* and it is doubtful if his proposed tax would in fact have shifted the tax burden from cities and farms and summer resorts to timberlands. He never had a chance to find out, however, because the timber owners of New Hampshire, stirring up

NRA lobbyists and hunters, took the lead in beating down his bills. The same is true in most states that have essayed statewide property taxes. To many moderns such taxes may appear novel and radical, but in fact in 1920 and before they were the mainstay of state-level revenues, not just of local revenues.

Dean Henry Vaux of the California State School of Forestry, Berkeley, in 1958 offered me an Assistant Professorship. I was not to ramble at will through the world of ideas, but to focus narrowly on the value of forest recreation — nothing about taxation. Vaux himself soon drafted California's Timber Preserve Zone (TPZ) Act, preempting forest land assessments from County Assessors and mandating use of a formula he worked out to assess forest land for taxation at about 10% or less of its true market value. Years later, when I had moved to U. C. Riverside, his son, Henry Vaux, Jr. played a key role in maneuvering to eliminate the entire Department of Economics, including my tenure — but not his. Hardly anyone but a few corporate CEO's would even know there was a TPZ, were it not for UCLA Law Professor Donald Hagman, a property tax expert and reformer of renown among urbanists. Hagman's great career was cut short when he fell off a cliff while jogging through Mendocino County, the heart of redwood *terroir*.

One could go on from state to state, but the bottom line is that Faustmann's great contribution to economic analysis, dating from 1849, died for over a century, was transfigured and reborn for a brief career after 1957, only to die again after a second life of about 20 years. When will it be born again? That is a question for present and future generations to answer.

— From a paper presented at the the Annual Meeting of the History of Economics Society, July 2010

Europe's Fatal Affair with the Value-Added Tax

———※◇❖———

In August, 2011, S&P lowered the credit rating of the US Treasury. We held our breath, thinking this might be the tipping point before a flight from the dollar. Congress, deadlocked and dysfunctional, seemed to deserve it — but it didn't happen. Mobile international capital saw something, spited S&P, and stayed with US Treasury securities. It seems that the USA must be doing something right — or at least less wrong than other nations. I would not breastbeat about "American Exceptionalism." I deplore our nation's faults, and our failure to face them and reform them. Nevertheless, it is foolish to preach that we must emulate Europe, when Europe is sliding downhill faster than we, and floundering as it slides.

I build a thesis around a simple, if partial, answer: the USA is the only major nation lacking a national-level sales tax (or VAT or GST). We raise a higher fraction of our combined national, state and local revenues from taxes on property, and income from property, and bequests of property. The fraction is not just a little higher, but plain to see even without the microscopes of modern theory and econometrics. (These myopic tools, indeed, often divert analysts into straining at gnats while they "swallow a camel.") True, our fraction of revenues raised from property has been trending downwards for half a century, but even so is still many times higher than in Europe, or in most nations of the world.

We'll consider how things got this way historically, in Europe and in the United States, and then explore the economics of just how bad an idea the VAT is.

History of a dumb idea

Before the Enlightenment, and the Ages of Reason and Benevolent Despotism, Europe raised revenues from excise taxes, tariffs, and tolls. It built roads with drafted *corvée* labor. In England, Thomas Hobbes, a leading influence on the Stuart Kings, had pushed hard for taxes on what he called "consumption" (although neither he nor any later sales-taxer, to my knowledge, has defined "consumption" carefully enough to give the concept a clear meaning). Slavery, serfdom, peonage, and indentured labor were common. Prison labor was not unknown. Underpaid religious staffed schools and hospitals, hospices and asylums.

French King Louis XVI, briefly playing the benevolent despot, in 1774 appointed Jacques Turgot his Finance Minister. Turgot was fresh from his triumphs as *Intendant* of *The Limousin* (Limoges), where his physiocratic reforms, intelligently conceived and conscientiously executed, had converted a stagnant province into a thriving one. The Physiocrats wrote and preached, and Turgot the statesman acted for untaxing commerce and industry and raising revenues from land taxation. They coined the slogan *laissez faire* for their philosophy.

While at Limoges, Turgot published his *Reflexions sur la Formation et la Distribution des Richesses* (1766). This short, compact work contains much of the essential wisdom that Adam Smith soon was to popularize and expand with *The Wealth of Nations* (1776). Turgot stressed the important roles of capital, and free markets. He favored letting the market determine interest rates. He would combat poverty by relieving the poor of taxes, while raising revenues instead from taxes on the value of land — including lands traditionally exempt or undertaxed. He correctly observed that taxes based on land values raise revenues without twisting and suppressing incentives to produce and invest. Smith visited France in 1766 and consulted extensively with Turgot, a man whose practical turn of mind made him a congenial tutor for Smith.

Adam Smith went on to ask why Spain, jump-started with gold pilfered from the New World, lagged in economic progress. He laid it on the Spanish *alcabala* and *cientos*: heavy sales taxes, their nominal rates magnified by cascading, that spared the grandees from taxes on their lands while stifling Spanish commerce and industry. They were just the sort of "broad-based" taxes which modern sales-taxers tout for raising more revenue, but under Philip II's *alcabala* and *cientos*, Spain declared national bankruptcy three times.

Many of America's "Founding Fathers" visited France as diplomats, and learned from Turgot. America's revolution against England meant friendship with France and Frenchmen. Turgot tried but failed to reform France in his day, but this French thinker and leader was one of our Founding Fathers in influence. The Commerce Clause of the US Constitution did for the new USA what Turgot had tried to do for France: it guaranteed free trade among the states. It created and has preserved our domestic market, the greatest free trade zone in the world, an essential ingredient of American productivity and prosperity.

However, in the new USA the Federalists under Hamilton first took control, and began levying excise taxes. In 1794 farmers of western Pennsylvania rebelled against a tax on their corn, which they marketed as whisky to cut down on transportation costs. Hamilton called on Federal troops to put down this uprising. The voters, when they found him dominating the subsequent cabinet of John Adams, and leading the country into the depression of 1798, retired his party and installed Jefferson, whose Virginia dynasty shaped the nation for the next 36 years.

These Virginians knew their Physiocracy. Jefferson, Madison and Monroe had all hobnobbed with philosophers in Paris and picked up their ideas. Monroe led the fight for the Commerce Clause, freeing internal trade from excise taxes. Jefferson's physiocratic agenda was extensive: he wrote the Northwest Ordinance dividing public lands for privatization in small parcels, bought Louisiana, brought the Physiocrats Gallatin and DuPont into his circle, welcomed Tom Paine back from France and extended easy credit to small buyers of western lands. It was Madison, with all his faults, who masterminded the Constitution, and then, in the War of 1812, used the Federal power to tax property (a power he had so carefully circumscribed). They got the new nation off to a flying start.

The Confederate states, even though fighting to survive, stood on their states' rights against their own CSA government, and bucked an attempted CSA property tax. Jefferson Davis had to finance secession with excise taxes. So Davis put a 10% tax on all farm production, paid in kind — a crushing burden on marginal farmers. Winn Parish, LA, for example (the home of Huey Long) in 1863 petitioned General Grant to save them from this "oppression." The CSA repudiated its bonds and currency, and lost the war catastrophically. Following attempted Reconstruction, however, came Hayes, Reunion and Restoration of the old ruling class which ever since, first as Democrats and now as Republicans, has saddled the old Confederate States with the most regressive tax systems in the nation, featuring heavy reliance on sales taxes.

Before lands acquired in the Louisiana purchase were sold out, President James K. Polk acquired more lands clear to the Pacific, our "Manifest Destiny," as he called it. The USA became the biggest free trade zone in history, and prospered mightily — albeit erratically and prodigally, with giant-swinging cycles of boom and bust. We tied the parts together with ambitious long rails, but financed them with land grants that spared us from taxes. When the nation annexed lands from France and Spain and Mexico it left the private titles intact, but freed them from the repressive tax systems of those nations. Americans old and new grew accustomed to low federal tax rates, over a long period. State and local governments performed most public functions, and lived mainly on property taxes, a kind of tax with no "taxable event" in its base and thus little, if any, disincentive effects.

Not until 1909 did the US turn to a corporation income tax, spurred by domestic demands for reform — and naval and military ambitions. The personal income tax from 1913 was carefully focused by Progressive Congresses on property income. Not until 1942 did Congress turn seriously to taxing wage and salary incomes, and withholding the taxes, and even then rates were graduated so steeply that property incomes, being in the top brackets, bore much of the brunt.

Since 1945 the tide has turned sharply back towards taxing labor more and property less, and yet even so America still taxes labor less, and property more, than most other nations. We stand alone — so far — as the nation with no national sales tax.

From Common Market to European Union and VAT

We pick up Europe's story in 1948. WWII left Germany devastated, but not for lack of money demand or purchasing power. Wartime rationing and price controls had left Germans with piles of cash in Reichsmarks. Ludwig Erhard, minister of finance under Konrad Adenauer, demonetized Hitler's Reichsmarks and replaced them with Deutschemarks as the new legal tender, lowering the effective money supply by 93%. German families lost not just capital goods, but their life savings. They were "ruined" — so it seemed. They didn't even have rationing tickets.

Erhard observed that the only rationing tickets they needed now were Deutschemarks, and they would work hard to get them. The same reasoning implies that they would also put their assets to work, if they owned any — and someone did own all the lands of Germany, and the surviving capital as well.

What followed was proclaimed a *Wirtschaftswunder*, but let us not call it a *Wunder* (miracle) for that suggests a supernatural cause, and stifles inquiry into real causes. It was unaccustomed

Armut (poverty) that drove Germans to perform. The first cause of poverty was the obvious: paying taxes to prepare for war, the total war itself, losing it, being bombed, then humiliated, occupied and plundered. Second, less obvious, was Erhard's repudiating Hitler's Reichsmarks. Economists who sympathize both with Erhard and private property may cover up the contradiction it by calling it "currency reform," but the naked fact is that Erhard's State simply stiffed its creditors, the German people, thus confiscating their private property without compensation. It came from recognizing that incentives come from *Morgen* (tomorrow) and are only dulled by the security and comfort of holding property in the accumulations of *Gestern* (yesterday). Yes, Erhard believed in free markets and incentives; decartelization and Walter Eucken and the Freibourg School were in vogue. Yes, Social Democrats discredited themselves by opposing Erhard, and it is good press to mock them for their doctrinaire myopia. But generations of conservatives since then have spun the story to blank out the role of state confiscation of private property.

Few would deny today that the desperate circumstances of the times necessitated radical "currency reform." Now that Erhard's policy is a *fait accompli*, safely in the past, few would deny its spectacular success. But let us learn the economic lesson. Taxes have two opposite kinds of effects. There are the marginal effects, the kinds that Laffer and a thousand anti-taxers preach, the disincentive effects of diluting the rewards of work and enterprise. But there are also the wealth effects, such as Erhard's "Miracle" demonstrated. Germany's experience suggests that the wealth effects may be stronger than the marginal effects. Certainly they are if we "play our cards right" and choose wisely among tax alternatives. The secret of raising revenues without damping incentives is to select kinds of taxes with powerful wealth effects and weak marginal effects. Property taxes come close to filling the bill, and even closer if we exempt capital improvements and movable capital (personal property) from the tax base. VATs, at the other pole, fit the Laffer model like a glove: strong effects on marginal incentives, and minimal wealth effects.

With the Marshall Plan the USA helped to rebuild Western Europe and Japan, with great success. "Social Democracy" was the slogan, to enlist proletarians in the common struggle against the Red Menace. Former belligerents buried the dulled hatchets of nationalism. French leaders like Jean Monnet and Robert Schuman proposed a United States of Europe, which would include the old Axis Powers, but not the USSR or its allies. France needed Germany to stop the USSR, and Germany was too big and robust for France to let go its own way again.

As the processes of European unification were getting underway, in the 1950s, the tide was turning back toward the attitudes of *l'ancien régime* with its taxes on merchants and their customers. Maurice Lauré, an engineer turned tax-man, got France to adopt VAT "to meet a fiscal crisis" (although that kind of spin accompanies most political moves). France introduced the first national VAT in 1954. It was not general, but was destined to become so, in 1968.

Charismatic Charles de Gaulle succeeded Coty, founded the 5th Republic, and presided from 1959-69. A fabled hero of *la résistance, Le Grand Charlie* could get what he wanted, and was President in 1963 when a Common Market committee on tax "harmonization" issued the landmark (Fritz) Neumark Report that found the French VAT to be superior to Germany's cascading turnover tax. The Committee agreed to make VAT the basis of tax harmonization within the growing EU. In 1968 France changed its VAT from partial to general.

Initial steps like European Coal and Steel Community and European Common Market grew to become the European Union. The 1957 Treaty of Rome created the European Community (EC), aka "The Common Market." In 1990 a commission led by former French Finance Minister Jacques Delors broached a single currency, a step short of political union. French President Francois Mitterand forced the Euro on a reluctant Germany as the price for France's support of German reunification after the Berlin Wall fell in 1989. The Maastricht Treaty of 1992 created the European Union (EU), which adopted the Euro. Soon the EU doubled in size, to 27 nations, including eight former members of the Soviet bloc.

VAT spread quickly around the world. To enter the European Union, member states were required to adopt it. Latin America also went along. In a second push around 1990, industrial states like Canada, Australia, Switzerland and Japan came on board too, along with many "developing" economies in Africa and Asia, until today some 140 nations use VAT. They were pushed along by newly empowered international organizations like OECD, the IMF and the World Bank — probably not what their founders had in mind at Bretton Woods in 1944.

The USA has played an anomalous role. The Shoup Mission to Japan in 1949 had tried to pioneer VAT there, although in vain. USAID has spent huge sums promoting and subsidizing VAT in small nations. Only the USA itself has rejected VAT. Evidently there is a wide gap between our international representatives and the voters at home.

Europe after VAT: troubles and setbacks

Today, in 2013, Europe is staggering. Many of its nations face bankruptcy. Its stronger members, and institutions they dominate, seek to impose "austerity" on the resentful weaker members. Its banks hold mostly its governments' securities, crowding out the small businesses that create most jobs. Its unemployment rates are breaking records. Its tax collections fall ever farther behind the needs, threatening both the governments and their bank-creditors with insolvency. Real estate manias in nations like Spain and Ireland, new to the perils of prosperity, have collapsed, bringing banks down with them.

The debts of Greece, Italy and Spain are in the headlines, but many "stronger" nations also owe more than their revenues can well handle. Greece owes $315 billion, but here are the debts of some "strong" nations, in billions of $US: Finland, 101; Austria 230; Belgium 374; Netherlands 427; and France 1,835. Even Germany, supposedly the EU's economic bulwark, began showing signs of stagnation in the 1990s, leading to the sarcastic epithet "The German Disease." Its debts are highest of all, at 2,086. The path of Germany's "Miracle" seems to be from unity and strength-through-defeat to disunity and weakness-through-success. Germany's claimed debt of about $2.1 trillion is rigged downwards by omitting huge pension obligations, estimated to add another $3 trillion to the total.

Governments' creditors are mostly banks, but these in turn are bailed out by the same governments to whom they lend, a spiral that will wind only downwards until and unless European governments find a way to raise tax rates without stifling tax bases. The whole structure rests, finally, on tax revenues; without them, it is just a house of cards. However, most tax bases fall when they are needed most, and the VAT base is falling fastest. In Greece, for example, public revenues have fallen 5% in the last year, while VAT revenues have fallen 15%. As credit ratings fall, required interest rates rise, so debt service rises, deficits rise, and debts keep growing, a disastrous vicious spiral. The expansion of the EU stopped late in 2012 when Bulgaria refused to adopt the Euro for fear it would be called on to bail out even weaker nations.

How did Europe and its fellow VAT nations reach this sorry state?

The economics of sales taxes: dubious virtues and real burdens

The idea keeps resurfacing that a sales tax is made neutral by virtue of being "general." Many great economists have refuted it, only to be inundated by floods of lesser voices in mass textbooks. Retail sales taxes, however "general" or universal in their apparent coverage, tax capital for turning over. Turnover is measured by the sales/capital ratio, which is highly variable among different firms, products, locations, stages of the cycle — and tax regimes, which economists influence. Sales taxes depress it heavily. This is not a mindless grouch at all taxes, for we need public revenues, and some taxes have positive effects. This is a rifle-shot at sales taxes, of which

VAT is one.

A major talking point among corporate spokesmen is that we must lower our corporate income tax rate, to make us "competitive" (today's buzzword). They give the impression that the income tax base is *gross* income. However, any income tax, personal or corporate, is less depressive, and has less excess burden, than any sales tax or VAT, however "general." That is partly because labor costs are deductible from taxable income. In addition, deducting capital outlays may lower the effective income tax rate on investing in new capital goods, often to zero and even below. As Turgot wrote, long ago, investing is "the beneficial and fruitful circulation that animates all the work of society...."

It is true that nominal corporate income-tax rates in the US have moved recently to the #1 rank among major OECD nations. That is not, however, because our rates have risen; rather, others have fallen. Italy's, for example, has dropped from 52% in 1962 to 27% in 2012, while Italy replaced the revenues by raising its VAT. If Italy had prospered, it might bolster the corporate lobbyists' argument. However, Italy has fallen to beggar status in the EU.

Today, US economists and pols of left and right are moving toward a pessimal consensus that lowering tax rates on business incomes (whose *rentier* components are not identified or quantified) is acceptable so long as Congress also closes "loopholes." Hardly anyone says *what* loopholes. It's important to realize that many loopholes, like fast writeoff and expensing of investing in creating new capital goods — genuinely "income-creating" spending — are exactly what made high rates of income taxation compatible with high rates of investing during the mid-20th Century.

Europe generally uses the "consumption-type VAT," meaning that capital outlays are expensible. This may have the effect of exempting the income of capital from the tax, although it is hard to find a comprehensible definition of "capital." If it includes land it is extremely discriminatory, and in any case favors more durable over less durable capital, and fixed over circulating capital. This should be a major issue, but it is untouched, to my knowledge, in the literature.

Modern writers deplore the exemption of "services" from the sales tax base. These writers and teachers refer in their contexts only to labor services, ignoring the service flows of land or capital. This is not from ignorance: they know that the "service-flow" of an owner's home has long been included in NIPA as a form of income, income consumed by the owner-occupant as the real estate yields it. They just blank that out when it comes to taxing services to the "final" consumer.

The Mill Effect

John Stuart Mill in 1848, citing an even earlier finding by John McCullough, showed that a seemingly "general" sales tax would tax capital for turning over, and thus induce investors to favor the kinds of capital goods that turn over slowly. In Austrian terms, the tax induces investors to lengthen the "period of production," and thus distort the "structure of capital" in favor of "high order" capital goods, such as buildings. In Austrian cycle theory, this is a cardinal sin of public policy. Modern Austrian writers, however, almost unanimously, blame the problem entirely on low interest rates enabled by misguided central bankers. Something is missing there, and that something is tax policy.

Here is Mill's proto-Austrian case against a general sales tax:

> "... if there were a tax on all commodities, exactly proportioned to their value, there would,... as Mr. M'Culloch has pointed out, be a 'disturbance' of values,... owing to the different durability of the capital employed in different occupations. ... In two different occupations ... if a greater proportion of one than of the other is fixed capital, or if that fixed capital is more durable, there will be less consumption of capital in the year, and less will be required to replace it, so that the profit, if absolutely the same, will form a greater proportion of the annual returns. To derive from a capital of £1,000 a profit of £100, the one producer may have to sell produce to the value of £1,100, the other only to the

value of £500. (I.e., where capital is less durable, you must sell more gross to get the same net profit.)

"If on these two branches of industry a tax be imposed... the one commodity must rise in price, or the other must fall, or both: commodities made chiefly by immediate labor must rise in value, as compared with those which are chiefly made by machinery.... " (Principles of Political Economy, *1848, Book V, Chapter IV)*

How memorable is Mill's word *"Disturbance,"* 150 years before Darth Vader sensed a Disturbance in The Force! In Mill's and McCulloch's usage, "The Force" is value as determined in a market before or without taxes based on gross sales.

What Mill means by "capital" is clear from his memorable saying, "Capital is kept in existence from age to age not by preservation but by continual reproduction." Capital is not a specific concrete good, like a chair in the furniture shop. Rather, it is a quantum of value that we can, and normally do, keep existing by using the cash from sales to "meet the next payroll," as they say, to replace the chair. It needn't be an identical chair, or any chair at all, for capital in this transition is totally fungible in form and location.

Within each business there are also differences among kinds of capital. In a retail bakery, for example, there are pies and pie-shelves. The pies come and go, perhaps several times a day; the shelves last for years; the ovens for decades; the buildings even longer; the sites forever. Many a needy widow with hardly any capital has earned her mite by baking, while renting the site, building and hardware. Her sales/capital ratio is high in contrast with that of the landlord, and orbital in contrast to, say, Georgia-Pacific or Weyerhaueser or Simpson or Ford's Roseburg timber corporations.

The case is even clearer when we compare two uses competing for the same land. Compare a parking lot with a cafeteria. Suppose both to be taxed on gross sales, including services. The inventory of fresh food in the cafeteria is taxed daily, as it sells out and turns over. The payrolls are taxed daily too, for they add to the gross value of sales. The value their labor adds to the purchased stock of food is capital, too: "working capital" — thus, the sales tax is mainly a tax on labor. The gross sales of parking lots, at the other extreme, include no turnover of capital at all, unless perhaps a minuscule Capital Consumption Allowance (CCA) on the paving and striping.

The business with more turnover pays more sales tax per dollar of capital invested. The tax drives away capital that turns over fast, and reallocates the land to capital that turns slower, or to uses requiring less capital, or no capital at all, like the parking lot. As to the lot itself, it never turns over in the relevant sense of wearing out and being replaced.

Curiously, many Georgists, though they are relentless critics of holding land idle, as well as of taxes with excess burdens, do not connect these two goals in one consistent system. Sales taxes inhibit using land intensively, if at all. Chemists have a good vocabulary for it. Land in production is like a chemical "catalyst" — it facilitates a process without disappearing into the product. Its "quantum of value" remains intact in the land. Working capital is, at the other extreme, like a "reactant." Its corpus and its quantum of value go into the product. That means they get sales-taxed with each turnover — the basis of the Mill Effect.

Hydraulic physics and engineering provide an excellent illustration, ably expounded by Robert Dorfman in a 1959 article I cannot praise too highly. Dorfman whimsically calls it "The Bathtub Theorem," and properly acknowledges Knut Wicksell's priority with his "grape-juice model." The average transit time of a molecule of liquid through a reservoir is basically the fund/flow ratio: in economic terms, the capital/sales ratio. For the lady baking pies and selling out daily the annual ratio is 1/365. For the boreal forester the annual ratio is 70 or more. The difference of 26,000 times starkly illustrates the Mill Effect. For doubters and masochists Dorfman provides many equations, but ends them delightfully saying "It is nice that this elaborate calculation is really unnecessary."

J. S. Mill hid this light under a bushel, offering just one example of a small difference, which was easy to overlook in passing — as later standard-brand economists have done. We should, rather, set this light in a tower on a hilltop as a beacon sending its gleam across the wave to save the foundering ship of state.

VAT and the Ramsey Rule

Most standard textbooks tell us that a truly general retail sales tax, unlike an excise tax, is neutral as between one commodity and another. A national tax is also neutral between locations, since it is the same in one region as another. Those conditions are never approached in practice, but in the sales-tax canon that merely means reformers should extend the reach of the tax, as the EU does with its push for tax "harmonization" among member nations, meaning in practice that all should adopt a VAT. Sales-taxers in the USA keep pushing for ways to override the Commerce Clause in the US Constitution and let each state tax imports from other states.

However, the Ramsey Rule says that in order to be allocationally neutral, sales tax rates should not be uniform at all, but inversely proportional to elasticities of supply and demand. As A. C. Pigou put it:

> If there is any commodity for which either the demand or the supply is absolutely inelastic, the formula implies that the rate of tax imposed on every other commodity must be nil, i.e. that the whole of the revenue wanted must be raised on that commodity.

Pigou's reasoning leads straight as a guided missile to levying taxes **exclusively** on the value of land, because its supply is inelastic. Whether Pigou knew what he was saying we may never know, for he was guarded and cautious and often coded, like so many academics fearful of witch-hunters.

Richard Musgrave avoids the issue by leaving Ramsey completely out of his classic *Theory of Public Finance*. Many, indeed most modern academics square the circle by first citing and then misquoting the Rule. They apply it only to *demand* elasticities — even though *supply* elasticities are clearly the more important part of the original rule. Allyn Young started this ball rolling in reviewing Pigou in 1929: "I shall assume that costs are constant. It will be unnecessary, therefore, to take account of elasticity of supply as something apart from elasticity of demand." The notable exception is Joseph Stiglitz, who often writes sympathetically of taxing land values.

More generally, sales taxes penalize high-volume low-markup marketing strategies as against their opposite.[*] Lest one turn up his nose at, say, Walmart, its low prices do not reflect low markup so much as low labor-service per dollar of inventory. It also provides acres of free parking, a service of land, like other big-box stores. Sullivan also notes that sellers in better locations, say Rodeo Drive, can have higher markups, so sales taxation favors pricier locations. New businesses with high startup costs can deduct them from taxable income, but not from gross sales. Clifford Cobb notes that ghettos have many barber shops and beauty parlors but few shops carrying commodities.

Down with sales taxes and VAT!

We are left with this: retail sales taxes tax capital for turning over. Turnover means replacement; and replacement sustains demand for labor. Replacement does not just depend on sales, it anticipates them, and thereby generates the consumer incomes that finance them. Turnover is the autonomous variable that takes the lead in the otherwise circular, and now vicious, circle of macroeconomics in which employers wait for consumers, while consumers wait for employers to hire them. Turnover is measured by the sales/capital ratio, which is highly variable among different firms, products, locations, stages of the cycle, and tax regimes. By taxing turnover, sales taxes shrink their own base. Arthur Laffer discredited this idea by letting his patrons apply it to all kinds of taxes; Murray Rothbard mistakenly applied it just to the property tax, the

---

[*] Dan Sullivan points this out in his article "Sales Tax Destroys Commerce, http://savingcommunities.org/issues/taxes/sales/destroyscommerce.html

one major tax to which it does *not* apply because it taxes capital and land for standing still, not for turning over.

Jobs depend on turnover. Sales taxes, rampant and rising in our times, depress turnover heavily, and this depresses demand for labor — both the number of jobs and their pay rates. Property taxes have the opposite effect, and so may some aspects of income taxation. Taxes on pure land value are the best of all. Our main point here, however, is that if the objective is to make jobs and raise pay rates, sales taxes (and their twin, VAT) are among the worst possible choices.

The idea that Europe has reached the limit of its taxable capacity is nonsense. The Cold War wound down from 1989. Today the USA, the only nation with no VAT, bears the cost of policing and defending Europe, and most of the world too. For centuries, Europe poured its treasures into a series of internecine wars from which the EU has rescued it. Europe now enjoys a colossal Peace Dividend, one of the biggest and longest in history. The idea that this should lead to national bankruptcies is absurd and ridiculous on its face. The alternative hypothesis is that Europe's woes are endogenous. A major cause, as shown earlier, is heavy reliance on VAT — the main tax to which Laffer's warnings might apply — and the lack of substantial taxes on property or its income. The evidence of Europe's solvency and untapped taxable capacity is the high level of its land prices compared with ours. International buyers are paying record-smashing figures for homes in world-class neighborhoods like Woodside and Los Alto Hills, San Mateo County, for example, because our prices, steep as they look to us, are still cheaper and the quality of life may be better than in counterpart regions of Europe.

— Working paper, www.masongaffney.org. Versions of this article appeared in Groundswell *and the* Georgist Journal.

Tom Jefferson
and the Dandelion

Thomas Jefferson is said to have introduced the dandelion in this country. No one's perfect. It's a shame, though, how some people seize on TJ's other lapses when his name is invoked, especially the rumor that he, an early widower, retained a slave mistress. This originated as a Federalist whispering campaign, and now it seems is probably true, but true or false, it is too prurient to die. To the racist, miscegenation compounds the fault. The salacious must be titillated, and if one upholds popular rights one will be slandered. Whether he treated her honorably, as apparently he did, is beside the point. Whether his enemies and critics engaged in similar behavior over the years is irrelevant. Egalitarians are held to a purer standard. Privileges are won by playing dirty, and that's how they are kept.

It is said that TJ should have freed his slaves. Apparently he considered it, but realized that a free black person in 18th century Virginia would not remain free, or perhaps even alive, for long. Social wrongs are hard for individuals to cure. What TJ did do was to exhaust his individual fortune in politics, giving him the power to enact the Northwest Ordinance creating our national land system, extend cheap credit to homesteaders there, bring French reformers to America, found the University of Virginia and design its campus, put the Bill of Rights in our Constitution, enact the Virginia Statute of Religious Freedom, outlaw primogeniture and entail, write the Declaration of Independence, help Tom Paine, edit the Jefferson Bible, and in many other ways help establish a fair and respectable American culture.

Politics makes strange bedfellows. In binding the national union together TJ allied with Robert Livingston, major landowner of the Hudson Valley. Livingston promoted income taxation to replace property taxation. A union-binder cannot demand perfection from all his friends — but the Livingston alliance troubles me. For a charming novel in the background of Livingston's age and place, try *Dragonwyck* by Anya Seton, or see the film with Vincent Price and Gene Tierney. It's a great one in a populist genre that would never make it today.

Then there are Gary Hart, Jimmy Swaggart, Jim Bakker and the rest of those Elmer Gantrys who stumbled on the Seventh Commandment. Hardly of the same class, but it is sad how justice became ethics, ethics became morality, and morality became monogamy. The Seventh Commandment became the single test of virtue, private and public, necessary and sufficient. On this and allied points, Kevin Phillips' recent book, *American Theocracy*, is a good read.

Violating The Ninth Commandment (slander) is the way of life in administration and the media. Violating The Sixth (murder) and Eighth (stealing) are the bases of land tenure, the royal road to riches, and through riches to respectability in church, academia, and society. Violating The Tenth (coveting) is confused with the instinct of workmanship and identified with the legitimate incentive to produce. Ostentatious charity, condemned by Jesus, is used to screen the rich from the working poor, select community leaders from the former, and shame and silence the latter.

Gore Vidal, who is no prude, has devoted an entire book to debunking Jefferson. One must take Vidal seriously here, since he is a serious scholar, yet you would expect him to sympathize with T.J.'s liberal spirit and broader aims. You might explain Vidal's hostility as a reaction to the military and imperialistic side of T.J.: writing the Second Amendment; founding West Point; sending the Marines to Tripoli; acquiring Louisiana; sending Lewis and Clark to promote expanding our empire to the Pacific; squelching Aaron Burr's scheme for an independent Mississippi Valley nation; and what not. This is not the place to review Vidal, but my impression is that the faults he cherry-picks are too petty to offset Jefferson's grander virtues and achievements.

So maybe Jefferson imported the dandelion. God forgives mortal sins; we can forget little ones. If all are God's children, and Earth is God's gift to His forgiven children, let's start over again with a Year of Jubilee. That means divide the land every fifty years, dandelions and all, as Moses said in Leviticus 25. (Billy Graham, Robert Schuler, Norman Vincent Peale, Jerry Falwell, Oral Roberts and Pat Robertson take note.) Or twenty-five, as Jefferson said. Either way we give each child of God a fresh start, "Ally Ally Oxen-free."

For the secular humanitarian, Jefferson imported another prolific European specimen, Pierre Samuel Du Pont (the first). Du Pont and his associates, the French school of *économistes*, founded classical economics. They also showed how to redistribute land rents daily, by taxing them. As they said, that makes us all "co-proprietors," and makes our children, and those of former slaves, continue as such, generation unto generation. Pierre Samuel IV, recently questing for Jefferson's former post, would have done well to reincarnate the practical egalitarianism of his namesake and progenitor, and of that man's friend and student, the Third President of the United States.

Corporations, Democracy and the US Supreme Court

⎯⎯⎯⎯⎯⊷◇⊶⎯⎯⎯⎯⎯

On Jan 21, 2010 our High Court shocked Americans by ruling in *Citizens United v. Federal Elections Commission* that a corporation may contribute unlimited funds advertising its views for and against political candidates. The ideas behind this are that a corporation is a "legal person" with all the rights of a human being; including that of donating money, which is a form of speech. This culminates a long series of actions and reactions (decisions, legislative acts, and electoral results) that bit by bit have raised the power of corporations in American economic and public life.

Some critics react apocalyptically, calling *Citizens United* a death blow to democracy; some cynically, calling this merely making *de jure* what is already *de facto;* some legalistically, saying the Court ruled more broadly than justified by the case brought before it. Supporters, naturally, take this contentedly as righting an injustice of long standing. Some economists would applaud this as a step toward sunsetting the corporate income tax, by electing more candidates beholden to corporate money. Many of them – not all – have been seeking this end for years in their learned journals and op-eds. Even the late William Vickrey, otherwise an egalitarian, gave high priority to this change.

I applaud neither sunsetting the tax, nor this step. I agree with Joseph Stiglitz that the corporate income tax is mainly a tax on economic rent. That means that a high tax rate does not destroy the tax base. It is not the ideal form of such a tax, but it beats any tax on work, or sales of the necessities of the poor, or value-added, or gross sales. Both Vickrey and Stiglitz rate high in the profession and garnered Nobels, so we cannot simply appeal to "authority." To prepare our minds, let us review some milestones in the history of corporations, especially in America.

My own postulates here, in brief, are 1) that corporations own a large fraction of the wealth in the country; 2) much of that wealth is land; 3) taxes that do fall on capital are in part shifted to land; 4) pure land taxes would, indeed, be better; and 5) payroll taxes are worse and must bear most of the burdens that are shifted off corporations.

Roman Law knew no such thing as corporate personhood. It grew in Europe after the 12th Century, to be used by bodies both civil (cities and guilds) and ecclesiastical, including universities. "The church" was a huge set of interlocking corporate bodies. Being immortal, corporations would progressively agglomerate land and power, leading to restrictions like the English Statutes of Mortmain (1279 and 1290), and direct attacks like confiscations as by Henry VIII. So, when America rebelled in 1776, Europe had had long experience with corporations and relevant law.

England, when it was our "mother country," gave the East India Company extraordinary powers. It was a private corporation acting as the "chosen instrument" of the Crown. The Company's powers included the governance of India, supported by the royal military; and a monopoly of tea export, enforced by the British Navy. Americans' early experience with this monopoly corporation was hostile: we were its angry exploited customer. Its monopoly power, coupled with Lord North's excise tax on tea, led of course to the "Boston Tea Party." The modern "Tea Party" seriously misinterprets this event, as a symbol to use against all taxes — while supporting politicians who support corporate monopolies. "It was the danger of this (tea) monopoly rather than the tax itself, only five pence to the pound, that aroused resentment in the colonies"[*]

---

[*] Henry Steele Commager, *Spirit of Seventy-Six.*

Some of the original 13 colonies were founded by chartered companies resembling corporations, with powers to grant land. A goal of the American Revolution was to strip these original governments of their corporate powers, and redistribute lands they had granted to their favorites. It was not the national government that confiscated Tory lands, but independent local militia seizing the occasion. Our "Minute Men" were the guerillas then. As John Adams said, "The Revolution was in the hearts and minds of men." The British controlled many major cities, but militia controlled the countryside, and made the most of it.

> *The girls in Boston are dancin' tonight;*
> *the gol-durned redcoats are holdin' em tight*
> *When we git there we'll show them how,*
> *but that ain't a-doin' us no good now*

What did "do them good" and motivate the militia was seizing lands from Tories. The Continental Congress had little tax power. Its currency fell to two cents on the dollar — "not worth a continental." Commander George Washington lost every battle against the redcoats until Yorktown. He was elsewhere when the Green Mountain Boys, organized to validate their "Wentworth" land grants, enabled General Horatio Gates to turn the tide at Saratoga:

> *Johnny Burgoyne in the wilderness,*
> *got his army in an awful mess*
> *The farmers got mad at the British and the Huns,*
> *and captured ten thousand son-of-a-guns*

It was southern militia that drove Cornwallis into his refuge at Yorktown:

> *General Washington and Rochambeau,*
> *drinking their wine by the firelight's glow,*
> *Big Dan Morgan come a-gallopin' in,*
> *we got Cornwallis in the old cowpen – (Soldiers' Joy)*

After the Revolution, naturally, Americans were not eager to restore the authority of colonial corporations. A common attitude in this era was that corporations are not persons because "they have neither souls to be damned nor bodies to be kicked"— they are outside and above social sanctions. Corporations are "soulless" and their directors' only social responsibility is to the shareholders (or, as it often turns out, to themselves and their top brass). The US Constitution did not mention corporations, leaving them to be chartered by the states, as they still are. It has been the US Supreme Court, using its power of judicial review, that gradually built up corporate power. The Constitution does not mention judicial review, either — it is a power that the Court, under Chief Justice John Marshall, gradually assumed from an early date and made into a tradition. Marshall was a Federalist politician and a disciple of Alexander Hamilton, whose chief concern was upholding "property," including property in land and slaves. Marshall was wily and took power effectively over a long tenure, 1801-35. His was the original "Activist Court" that propertied people have always supported (until it briefly became a pejorative to be used against the Warren Court).

The next milestone was the decision in *Trustees of Dartmouth College v. Woodward*, 1819. The Governor of New Hampshire, William Plumer, and his Legislature sought to take control of Dartmouth College to turn it from an elite private institution into a public university for a wider student body. Dartmouth had been founded by Eleazar Wheelock in 1769 under a corporate Charter from King George III — not a popular name in America. The original purpose was to "save" and instruct the Indians in European ways like drinking rum and privatizing lands.

> *Oh, Eleazar Wheelock was a very pious man*
> *He went into the wilderness to teach the Indian*
> *With a gradus and a Parnassum, a Bible and a drum*
> *And five hundred gallons of New England rum.*
> *— (Dartmouth student song)*

Governor Plumer believed that the Revolution had transferred sovereignty from the King to American legislatures, so he might take control by appointing new trustees. Daniel Webster, representing the trustees, prevailed upon John Marshall to validate King George's charter on the grounds that a privilege, once given, was a contract in perpetuity and could not be withdrawn. The effect on academic freedom was to subject faculty members completely to the will of self-perpetuating boards of trustees. The effect on privileges was to give them *sanctity* — however they originated and whatever damage they do to society at large. Before that the grant of a corporate charter was seen as a *privilege*, not a right; it was not property, but something more like a license to sell liquor or cut hair. It was subject to conditions, and revocable without compensation. After *Dartmouth* it had the best of both worlds: it was still not taxable as property, but otherwise protected under the 5th and later 14th Amendments.

In 1832 Andrew Jackson defied the High Court in *Worcester v. Georgia*. Apparently Jackson never actually said "Marshall has made his decision, now let him enforce it" as often quoted, but that was the idea. Jackson was morally wrong, by modern values – he and Georgia aimed to force the Cherokees from their ancient homeland. The point for us here, though, is that Jackson prevailed, demonstrating that a strong, assertive President can face down a Chief Justice when he thinks the stakes are high enough. This is relevant today: *Citizens United* has indeed raised the stakes high enough.

The next legal milestone was the dreadful *Dred Scott* decision by Roger Taney's Court, 1857. *Dred Scott* demonstrated two things we should note today. One is the tendency of the Court, left to its own devices, to uphold "property rights" of whatever kind, even in human flesh, in disregard of human rights like personal freedom. The other is the tendency of median Americans to react against the Court when it overreaches.

The reaction to *Dred Scott* produced, besides an awful war, The Emancipation Proclamation in 1863. This was an extra-legal act that Lincoln felt strong enough to perform after Union troops blocked Lee's invasion at Antietam, and no slave-owner felt strong enough to challenge as invading the "sanctity of property" and no Court to review. Following the war came the Radical Republican Congress that pushed Reconstruction in the South, and the 13th, 14th and 15th Amendments establishing the freedmen as citizens with full rights. These were radical acts under radical leaders like Thaddeus Stevens, leading towards considerable taxation of real estate in the south, temporarily.

Next came the Grant Administration, 1869-77, filled with bribery scandals and giveaways of public lands to private corporations, mainly to build railways. The Desert Land Act of 1876 also rationalized a giveaway of vast lands plus the Kern River, supposedly to promote irrigation. Mark Twain and Charles Dudley Warner labeled it "The Gilded Age" (the first one), and "The Great Barbecue." Greed in corporate forms rushed in to exploit the sacrifices of millions of soldiers in the bloodiest war in US history.

In 1871 an obscure San Francisco journalist, Henry George, published *Our Land and Land Policy*, with a map showing the extent of the railroad land grants, painting them as broad swaths comprising a large fraction of the west. Historians like Paul Gates now credit him with being first to sound the alarm, slowly resulting in various political reactions like the Populist, Progressive, and Single Tax movements.

Meantime, propertied northerners recaptured the Republican Party and joined forces with propertied southerners to install Rutherford Hayes as President in the disputed election of 1876. Thus ended Reconstruction and Radical Republicanism.

In 1873 came a great crash, starting a ten-year depression that slowly turned minds against corporations and the enormous land grants that the "robber barons" controlled. These bided their time until recovery and complacency let our High Court rule in *Santa Clara County v. The Southern Pacific Railroad*, 1886, that the corporation was a "legal person" within the meaning of the 14th Amendment. The Court hijacked the Amendment, passed to protect the rights and properties of former slaves, to protect corporations. The tenures deriving from the notorious bribery scandals of the Grant years were now above the reach of any state.

The reaction to the *Santa Clara* kind of judicial activism was voter receptivity to another wave of reform. History books dwell on changes at the Federal level during The Age of Reform, led by the Populist and Progressive Movements; but the unsung part of reform was that states, cities, counties and school districts struck back at land barons by raising state and local property taxes to finance public schools and public works of many kinds. 1880-1920 was the golden age of urbanization in the USA, and growing cities taxed property to provide schools to make people literate, and many services like sanitation and water supply to make urban life possible. Henry George and his followers were leaders of this movement.

At the Federal level many dissidents joined to form The Populist Party, who won a million votes and 22 electoral votes in 1892 for their little-known presidential candidate, James Weaver. Two years later they polled 50% more votes. They elected six senators and several congressmen and enough influence to pass a desired progressive personal income tax that included a tax on property income. In 1896 they merged with the Democrats, cast out old leaders like Cleveland and went with Bryan and his brain, John Peter Altgeld. Republicans, trolling for their votes, became Progressives themselves under T. Roosevelt and Wm. H. Taft, followed by Progressive Democrat Wilson, so for two decades, we had two Progressive Parties. Many Progressive Republicans and their ideas even survived the postwar reaction against Wilson. Few have called Andrew Mellon, powerful Treasury Secretary who virtually ruled Presidents Harding, Coolidge and Hoover, a Progressive — and yet he wrote in 1924, in *Taxation: the People's Business,* that we should tax property-derived income higher than wage income.

Of course in 1894 our High Court had overturned the Populist personal income tax on the grounds that it included a tax on real estate income, which they construed as a "direct" tax (*Pollock v. Farmers' Loan and Trust Co.*). The U.S. Constitution reads that a "direct" tax must be apportioned among the states according to population. This setback, however, only led first of all to the corporate income tax of 1909, a major blow to corporations, and then in 1913 to the 16th Amendment and the personal income tax. In 1916 the first substantial income tax bill under the amendment exempted most wage and salary income, making this more a tax on property income even than envisioned in the Act that the 1894 Court had disallowed.

By 1917 the old Populists could say they had achieved most of their goals through other Parties. The postwar reaction of 1920, however, was all the Court needed to rule in *Eisner v. Macomber*, 1920, that the IRS could not tax unrealized capital gains without another Act of Congress — an Act that Congress never provided. This has provided a major loophole ever since, both for corporations and their shareholders.

Meantime in England a parallel movement led by the "Radical-Liberals" installed in series three Prime Ministers: Henry Campbell-Bannerman, Herbert Asquith, and David Lloyd-George. In 1909 Lloyd-George, then Chancellor of the Exchequer under Asquith, introduced his radical "Peoples' Budget" including a token tax on the hitherto untouchable ancestral lands of the Lords. When the House of Lords vetoed it, Asquith demonstrated how a strong executive can overawe such a body: he prevailed upon King Edward VII to threaten to "pack" the House by creating new peers. The Lords bowed to superior fire power and passed the budget — an event known since as the Constitutional Revolution in England. Americans were watching.

In 1937 President FDR, at the height of his electoral strength, tired of having the High Court reject his programs. He copied Lloyd-George's 1909 success against the House of Lords. He didn't just threaten to "pack" the Court by adding new justices; he played hardball with the Reorganization of Judiciary Act. This did not go down easily and a major battle loomed, when Justice Owen Roberts, who had been joining in 5-4 majorities against the

President, prudently changed sides in a minimum wage case. It's been called "the switch in time that saved nine" (cutely mimicking an old saying that many young people today have never heard). It demonstrated that there are limits to the Court's power to override a united electorate.

All along, though, an accumulation of small actions was helping corporations at the expense of labor. The Warren Court, 1953-69, did many notable deeds for the common man and woman, but it did not stop the decremental fall of the share of corporate income tax revenues in Federal finance. In 1968 the payroll tax quietly surpassed the corporate tax as the second biggest source of Federal Revenue. Just think: the corporate income tax of 1909 antedated the payroll tax of 1935 by 26 years, and it was another 33 years, 1935-68, before the payroll tax took in more money than the corporate tax did. That was a revolution indeed, but so quiet and gradual that most people never noticed. Nor was that the end of it: by 2008 the corporate tax raised just 11% of Federal revenues, compared with 38% for the payroll tax, nearly 4 times as much. That is a measure of the growing power of corporations in politics.

On top of that, *personal* income taxes on corporate dividends and capital gains have been singled out for preferentially low rates. In 2003 President Bush and his Congress lowered the tax rate on both dividends and capital gains to 15%, so that a smaller share of the personal income tax now comes from corporate shareholders. As late as in the Tax Reform Act of 1986, dividends were taxed like other "ordinary" income. So, briefly, were capital gains. President George H. W. Bush then devoted most of his presidency, and sacrificed a second term, to get a token cut in the capital gains rate. It was the thin end of a wedge, leading soon to the present cap of 15%. "Capital gains" so-called by Congress, derive from many sources, but one of the biggest is sales of corporate stock.

And so things stood until January 21, 2010, when the High Court authorized corporate leaders to contribute unlimited amounts of their shareholders' cash to political causes. This poses a challenge to our tabloid-and-TV-numbed generation. Will "ordinary" taxpayers rebel, as they did in the American Revolution, Emancipation, the Progressive Age of Reform, and the New Deal? Or will corporate power wax unchecked until it replaces democracy altogether? Cyclical theory says we will have another anti-corporate reaction, but history also records tipping points in the decline of nations from which they do not recover for generations, if ever. This one may be a squeaker.

— Adapted from the article that appeared in Groundswell,
January–February 2010

The Top Ten Problems with "Corporate Personhood":

1. Corporations never die, never pay estate taxes, never divide their wealth among succeeding generations. In this they resemble medieval Churches that agglomerated over many years so much land they threatened the state itself.

2. Besides not dying, corporations merge with or otherwise acquire other corporations, progressing, if unchecked, from competition to cartel to oligopoly to monopoly.

3. A corporation is by nature a combination in restraint of trade – that is, a union of many individuals with their wealth to act as a unit, dealing with customers, suppliers, and workers. The courts, historically, have borne down on labor unions as illegal combinations — while treating this combination of lands and capitals as an individual.

4. Corporations enjoy the legal privilege of limited liability.

5. The ownership of corporations is very often secret. Many stocks are recorded in "street names." Hugo Chavez is one such owner whose name has been revealed: others might be Al Qaeda, the Nazi Party, the heirs of Mao Tse-Tung, La Cosa Nostra, or anyone. No citizenship is required for a corporation to sway American government more than any private citizen.

6. No person is easily held responsible for corporate acts. The first duty of CEOs is to the shareholders, so they say, to dodge guilt for any outrage against others. Most shareholders, in turn, have little idea what their CEOs are doing.

7. The internal governance of most corporations is intensely undemocratic.

8. The corporation cannot be jailed, and its officers seldom are, as they have great opportunities to pass the buck.

9. The corporation has no spiritual counselor or confessor to prick its conscience.

10. Before *Citizens United,* the attitude, as expressed by Justices White and Rehnquist in the 1970s, has been that corporations are "creatures of the law," not equal to natural persons in their civil rights. Suddenly to reverse this now is to upset many expectations that relied on the previous rule.

— Georgist Journal, *Autumn 2012*

Reverberations

⟫◦⟪

We begin with the Pecora Hearings of March 1933 — ten days that shook Wall Street. These were the dying days of Herbert Hoover's Administration and the Republican Congress. Hoover was desperate to hold back safely short of challenging the cartelization of American industry he had sponsored. So, he pushed the lame duck Senate's Banking and Currency Committee to investigate Wall Street and gin up some scapegoats to save Hoover's face and reputation. Chair of the Committee, through Senate seniority rules, was Peter Norbeck of South Dakota, a residue of old prairie Populism via Teddy Roosevelt's Bull Moose Party, and an unreconstructed Progressive. Norbeck, who knew little of Banking and Currency, sought a savvy prosecutor for the hearings.

Few wanted the job — two weeks working for a lame duck Congress, making powerful enemies. Far down on his list Norbeck came to Ferdinand Pecora, a mere assistant D.A. for New York County. Pecora likewise knew little of banking and currency, but was a quick study with remarkable energy, high ambition and little awe of pedigreed bankers with Ivy League degrees. Pecora pushed his inquiries well beyond what Hoover had dreamed, and forced so many famous bankers to disrobe under oath that the hearings made banner headlines — and are still known by his name.

Pecora had only ten days to put Wall Street under oath, but

he seized the public spotlight with his sense of drama and his aim for big players and big issues. Pecora's ten days preceded FDR's 100 days, and built a springboard for New Dealers to vault into reforms like the SEC, the FDIC, the RFC*, Glass-Steagall, production credit for farmers, and federal intervention in credit markets through FHA, S&L subsidies, FNMA, and later the VA.

Before Pecora, bankers were already under fire for bad judgment; after Pecora, they were "banksters," disgraced for bad faith, breach of trust and self-dealing. Several were to face criminal charges. Pecora dislodged bankers from their economic, political and social pedestal atop high society and government bureaucrats, and turned the world of finance upside down. FDR could not have asked for a better springboard.

Not since the Pujo Committee revelations of 1912-13, and Louis Brandeis's classic book thereon, *Other People's Money*, both at the acme of the Progressive Era, had anyone penetrated so deeply through Wall Street's opacity to publicize its villainies. Nor, tragically, has anyone done so since.

There was, however, a lacuna in Pecora's brilliant performance. He saw the Great Crash as mainly a matter of money and securities — the paper economy, if you will. This view has narrowed and confined reformers ever since. Macroeconomics has become synonymous with Fiscal and Monetary Policy (FMP). The template is $Y = C+I+G$.† Everything is expressed in its terms — it dominates language, and thought. "The Left" wants more C and welfare G; "The Right" wants more I and military G. Within those confines the same tired sermons echo back and forth endlessly. This is its own kind of "reverberation," but not the kind my title means. This is the long-term effect of Pecora's lacuna.

One major change came along with Reagan-Cheney and their

---

* The Reconstruction Finance Corporation, an independent agency of the United States government, established by the US Congress in 1932. — *Ed.*

† A standard expression of Gross Domestic Product (GDP). The variables are C, consumption; I, investment and G, government spending. — *Ed.*

Laffer staffer after 1981. "The Right," long a bulwark against deficit finance, converted to it. Instead of taxing the rich, the idea was now to borrow from them, and pay them interest. This led to an explosion of Gini Ratios in real estate, stocks, bonds, income (personal and corporate), estates, and nearly anything that gets measured. It's gone so far that we need nothing as subtle as a Gini Ratio: now it's the 1% vs. the 99%.

Meantime, other scholars published a distinguished body of research into matters of the real economy — but the academic clerisy has purged most of these from macroeconomics by compartmentalization. One may only study them within accepted confines. When submitting work for publication one is required to self-classify it by pigeonhole, taken from a standard list. There is an implicit hierarchy of little boxes, with Macro on the "commanding heights."

The clerisy sanitizes macro from contamination from:

a. *Real estate and its endogenous cycle of about 18 years,* firmly documented from primary sources and established by Homer Hoyt in his classic, *100 years of Land Values in Chicago, 1833-1933.* Other writers reinforced and replicated the findings: Ernest Fisher and John J. Holland in Michigan, Phillip Cornick in New York, H.D. Simpson in Chicago, Lewis Maverick on subdivision cycles, Arthur H. Cole on cycles in sales of public land, Harry Scherman on foreclosures, and others.

Hoyt carried this back no further than 100 years because there was no Chicago before 1833, but 18 years before Chicago's and Andrew Jackson's great crash of 1836-37 there was Monroe's crash of 1819, and 21 years before that was Hamilton's crash of 1798. Andrew Jackson lost his lands in that one, and William Morris and William Duer went to debtors' prison. Before that one can find crash before crash in the annals: the Mississippi Bubble of 1720; the Dutch crash of 1630 or so, synchronized with the reverse migration from New England after 1630; in the 15th Century it was the Fugger bank in Augsburg that went down with the fortunes of imperialistic Spain; the Florentine and Medici-banker bust of 1494 leading to Savonarola's Bonfire of the Vanities; boom and bust around Orleans following its liberation by Joan of Arc in 1429; and so on.

Apart from the endogenous 18-year cycle, major peace treaties can be shown to generate irrational exuberance for future land rents, and to release funds to the private sector where they are used again to bid up land prices. The interplay of these two cycles explains much of cyclical economic history.

b. *Austrian economics,* analyzing causes and effects of the time-structure of capital and the pace of capital turnover. Oddly, many economists who should know better identify Hayek with the Chicago School because he once taught there, but he was never welcomed in the Department of Economics. Frank Knight's many learned articles attacking Hayek's capital theory were an obsession, carrying on J.B. Clark's vendetta against Eugen von Böhm-Bawerk. Knight, like Clark, could not abide the Austrians' concept of a "period of production" because it implies a sharp distinction between capital goods, which have one, and land, which does not.

Hayek and fellow Austrians finally found happiness and support with libertarian foundations and other wealthy patrons, by attacking regulations and contra-cyclical fiscal policies of all kinds, to the applause of Chambers of Commerce, but they remain outliers in the profession.

c. *Institutional economics,* the heritage of Veblen, Commons, Ayres, Montgomery, Means, Thurman Arnold, Corcoran and Cohen, the TNEC investigations, and Senator Harry Truman's hearings on arms profiteering in the early 1940's. Dominant figures in the FMP camps, both Keynesian and Chicagoan, diss and dismiss such work by compartmentalizing it as mere "structural reform," unworthy of attention in the greater world of $Y = C + I + G$. Studies of industrial organization and cartelization and market power have dwindled to a shadow, although Joe Bain, Frederick

Scherer and others produced excellent texts on the subject.

The obvious link between FMP and real estate is the quality of credit. Hoyt emphasized how subprime (which he called "shoestring") financing had waxed in the boom phase of every one of the five major land cycles he documented in detail from 1833 to 1933. The commercial loan school of banking, dominant in the Progressive Era, helped save us from a crash that was due in or near 1911, following the 18-year cycle from 1893. In the roaring 1920s such old-fashioned caution was cast aside, and deposit expansion was again used freely to pump up land and stock prices. These reverberated with deposit expansion, in the manner to be shown, leading to The Great Real Estate Crash starting from 1926, followed by the stock crash of 1929.

Yet, Friedman and his school of "monetarism" ruled this out of consideration. They damned Quality Control as bureaucratic "intervention" with private bankers. Only Quantity Control was permissible. Ignoring Pecora's revelations, Friedman *et. al.* knew that profit-seeking bankers, proven survivors in free markets, must possess sounder judgment than nosy governmental officers. Pecora's findings were not refuted or denied — that would remind people of them. They were just quietly ignored.

What kept us out of serious trouble for so long? After 1945, nearly everyone forecast a postwar depression. The standard FMP line was (and is) that only wartime spending had jolted us out of the Great Depression, and peace would spoil the party. This postwar gloom capped land prices. Land for housing and farming was affordable; young entrepreneurs and home buyers could borrow to buy cheaply. Loans were mostly for production and use; price/earnings ratios ran low, payoffs were fast. All kinds of taxes remained high, stifling any kind of long-term irrational exuberance, and any "Reverberations" between land prices and bank expansion, *á la* the 1920s.

Soon came the Cold War, the Korean War (1950-53), the

costly Interstate Highway Program, urban sprawl with need for new infrastructure, the boom in airports, California's Central Valley Project and Water Plan, huge new "Big Dam Foolishness" and reservoirs on the Colorado, Missouri, Tennessee and Saint Lawrence Rivers, all costing huge sums and presaging continued high taxes, meaning continued low land prices. Politically and socially, the disgraces of Senator McCarthy, Spiro Agnew, and Richard Nixon, along with social programs supported by the Warren Court, presaged more social spending and continued high taxes of all kinds. The result was to keep stifling irrational exuberance and resulting high land prices.

As to credit, S&Ls got favored access to housing lending, keeping banks of deposit in their proper place. These banks were fed a steady diet of Treasuries, considered "non-defaultable," keeping them out of real estate which had proven so unstable before.

What are these "Reverberations" that led to the crashes of 1929 and 2008, with lesser ones in between, and earlier to the 18-year cycles of the 19th and earlier centuries? The basic process goes like this:

☞ Something sparks recovery and growth, such as a peace dividend following a major peace treaty: the Mississippi Bubble followed the Peace of Utrecht, 1713; the first railroad boom followed the Treaty of Guadalupe-Hidalgo, 1848; the second such boom followed Lee's surrender in 1865; the boom of the 1920s followed the Peace of Versailles. It also helps when a polity has "magnetic" institutions that attract people and capital, and/or a vast reservoir of empty lands to fill.

☞ Banks of deposit begin to shift from commercial loans, short-term and self-liquidating, to lending on real estate collateral for longer terms.

☞ This surge of new demand raises land prices.

☞ Rising land prices evoke prospects of further rises, and a new kind of demand for land — no longer just for early use, but for "investment," i.e. for a "store of value," for resale, for flipping, and for speculation of various kinds. In a rising market, this often surpasses and outweighs the discounted cash or service flow from current use.

☞ With higher prices, buyers need bigger loans and longer terms to pay for the same land. Banks create new demand deposits, taking the higher-priced land as collateral, and so on back and forth: *Reverberating,* bouncing back and forth many times.

☞ It's not only new buyers who use land as collateral. Old owners borrow on the swollen collateral to spend more on consuming.

☞ There is no rise of production, just a rise of prices of the same land.

☞ With longer-term loans, loan turnover falls, making new loans harder to get. Credit ratings fall, regardless of recorded interest rates, so the pool of eligible borrowers falls even as the supply of loanable funds falls as well. Demand for land is lowered by this shrinkage of available credit.

☞ The upward spiral turns downward. Reverberations become negative. A cumulative crash follows.

Why do land prices have to fall?

Land is fixed, leading to a belief that effective supply is fixed as demand rises. This is illusory, because access to land for higher (more intensive) uses expands into wide open spaces. There are dozens of stages of more intensive use: from hunting and fishing to trapping, from lumbering to tree farming, from that to sheeping to beef cattle, from grazing to feeding, to farming small grains to maize, to horticulture, to irrigation, to vines and groves and orchards, to country estates, to subdivisions and housing, to low-rise apartments, to commerce and industry, to high-rise condos and offices and hotels, with many stages of intensity along the way.

J.S. Mill's *Principles* has a chapter on "Influence of the Progress of Industry and Population on Rents, Profits and Wages." In Article Four of this Mill stresses that progress may be land-saving, not just labor-saving and land-using. Mill said that growth of population lowers wages, but progress in the arts may offset this, and may even raise wages. When labor is dear, capital goes into saving labor; when land is dear, capital goes into saving land, and developing new lands.

Credit is due rather to the arts of architecture, construction, planning, and engineering that crafted the elevators, ventilators, pumps, central heating, load-bearing supports, plumbing and sanitation, etc. Men taught themselves these arts, by the way, in deep mines before they used them to build skyscrapers — we learned to build up by building down into our home, The Earth. (May economic theorists profit by the example.) Thus the system is more self-equilibrating than many later writers and investors have assumed, but this occurs over such a long cycle that rational perceptions often give way to irrational exuberance.

Fully built-out towns like, say, the Milwaukee near-in suburbs of Shorewood and Whitefish Bay, house 10,000 people per square mile in spacious comfort in single-family homes on tree-lined streets with curbs, gutters, parkways, and sidewalks, with parks and golf courses and even a band of mansions along the lake shore. At that density the US population of 300 million souls needs 30,000 square miles, an area contained in a circle with radius of 100 miles — do the math. One hundred miles exceeds the distance from downtown to the outlying suburbs of any major city today, and 30,000 square miles is just about the area of South Carolina. The USA only seems crowded because of institutional biases that make us substitute land for labor and capital, and that gum up the land market.

These biases lead to territorial expansion. The kind most observed is urban sprawl, spreading cities and their infrastructure over many times more land than they need. Underuse of the best lands pushes settlement out to inferior lands, connected by capital tied up in infrastructure, premature in time and scattered over space.

Along with simple urban sprawl there is continental sprawl, urged on by works like the Interstate Highway System, interregional transfers of water, oil, gas, electric power, and the network of airlines and airports.

When did the 18-year endogenous cycle resume after 1945?

The incipient peace dividend following the surrenders of Germany and Japan hardly got started when the Cold War intervened, plus a hot war in Korea, 1950-53. There was no scope for a peace movement like that of 1918-38 when Mellon could hold down tax rates and pay down the national debt at the same time, feeding capital into the private sector by a process of "reverse crowding-out."

New capital in the private sector might seem like a key to prosperity. However, we saw above that in practice it triggers off the "Reverberation" process described above — so prosperity carries the seeds of its own crash.

After 1953 there was a bit of slack for a mild boomlet, damped, however, by gnawing fears of an inevitable nuclear holocaust. Hard as it is to believe today, many people spent big money digging and lining and provisioning bomb shelters in their back yards. John von Neumann, pioneer computer genius and "game theorist," was advising Presidents Truman and Eisenhower to wage "preventive war" against the USSR.

Following the damped 'fifties, came a headier boom in the "soaring sixties" with JFK's morale-lifting face-off with Krushchev in the Cuban missile crisis. Ike's Interstate Highway program, intended to link cities, was used to facilitate white flight and urban sprawl. Heller's form of "business Keynesianism" created a deficit by allowing fast write-offs on new investing rather than by raising spending. LBJ promised a "Great Society" with Civil Rights and a War on Poverty, but it ended in a funk with Viet Nam, the OPEC embargo, gas lines, rampant environmentalism, Brown's "Age of Limits," urban riots, urban "removal" in lieu of renewal, Watergate, and The Phillips Curve. High tax rates tempered the amplitude of the cycle, but the period was about the same old 18 years.

In about 1973 a new upsurge of land prices began. Nixon had declared "We are all Keynesians now," and Republicans, traditional

budget-balancers, faced about gradually to embrace both devaluation and deficit finance. President Reagan, campaigning on Laffer's
Curve and Cheney's military-industrial complex, took deficit finance
to new heights. Cheney, embracing Robert Barro's new theories and
Sargent's "rational expectations," memorably declared that "Deficits
don't matter." Even Milton Friedman, the prime anti-Keynesian and
monetarist guru, endorsed Barro's new rationale for deficit spending.
It was Democrat Fritz Mondale, challenging Reagan in 1984, who
urged balancing the budget — and lost.

This new upsurge, untempered and uncapped, led to the Crash
of 1990, a big crash, reminiscent of Hoyt's 19th century Chicago
history. With remarkable facility and amnesia, however, Americans
promptly forgot its obvious lessons and launched eagerly into the
next cycle, deregulating everything in sight by underfunding the
regulatory agencies, and dismantling most of the New Deal reforms.
President Clinton provided the cover of a Democrat in office, but
his policy of "triangulation" and "reverse crowding-out" merely deferred the debt skyrocket that went wild from 2001-09.

The period 1990-2008 saw a perfect 18-year cycle of peak,
crash, recovery, boom and another bust in real estate, right out of
Homer Hoyt's playbook. Cause and effect reverberated back and
forth between soaring land prices and expanding bank deposits.
Congress repealed Glass-Steagall in 1998, and Clinton signed on.
Banks loaned loosely and freely on mortgages, and invented many
new ways to securitize them, concealing the underlying collateral
under pyramids of paper with misleading and confusing new names.
Capital flowed southwestwards from rustbelt regions to growth regions like California, where Prop 13 had removed the former tem-
pering effect of property taxes. In Riverside, California, land prices
rose about 8-fold, 1990-2008 — heady stuff for householders and
other landowners who could cash out without even selling, by using
lines of credit, "living high on the old homestead."

Where were leading economic forecasters and advisers during the runup to 2008? Most of them were chanting "This time is

different!" The *Washington Post*'s main source on the housing market was David Lereah, chief economist for the National Association of Realtors, who also penned a 2006 bestseller *Why The Real Estate Boom Will Not Bust and How You Can Profit From It*. Michael Mandel, Chief Economics Editor of *Business Week*, published *Rational Exuberance: Silencing the Enemies of Growth and Why the Future is Better than You Think*. The White House Budget Director, Jim Nussle, declared that the nation had "avoided a recession." Ben Bernanke said we had entered "The Great Moderation." "The troubles in the subprime sector seem unlikely to seriously spill over to the broader economy or the financial system," he said on June 5, 2007. Christina D. Romer, Obama's first pick to chair his Council of Economic Advisers, proclaimed that we had "conquered the business cycle."

What are the prospects for another endogenous 18-year cycle, peaking and crashing in about 2026? Will they ever learn? Not yet, apparently, because now in 2012 politicians, bankers and land speculators are already seeking to start again on the same trajectory, the only route to "prosperity" they know. Already The Rijksbank has awarded the latest Nobel in economics to Thomas Sargent, the "rational expectations" man. Public policy at every level is bent to sustain and revive land prices, equated with recovery and prosperity. Banks "too big to fail" are bailed out, and no bankers jailed. Summers' friend Tim Geithner remains Treasury Secretary. There are no signs of remorse, of lessons learned.

We need a new Ferdinand Pecora, and a renewed sense of moral indignation *á la* FDR — and we need a new sense of the key role of land pricing in macro cycles. Land economics must be re-integrated with macroeconomics, so establishmentarians can at last begin to connect the dots.

— Georgist Journal, *Spring 2012*

Henry George:
the Great Reconciler

——————⇒▷◇◁⇐——————

Henry George (1839-1897) is best known today for *Progress and Poverty* (1879). Eloquent, timely and challenging, this book soon became and remains the all-time best-seller on economic theory and policy.

In 1879, George electrified the world by identifying one underlying cause for two great economic plagues: chronic poverty arising from insufficient demand for labor, and cycles of boom and bust. These twin plagues arose from concentrated ownership of land, compounded by land speculation. Large landowners and speculators held the best land idle or underused, forcing labor onto marginal land and driving down wages. Collapse of speculative land price bubbles caused periodic slumps. (By "land" George meant exclusive rights to use natural resources in a specified territory. It included mining, water, fishing, and timber rights, road and rail rights-of way, and some patents. George emphasized the high value and productivity of urban land, which facilitated communication and trade. Today, we would add to "land" such items as telecommunications licenses, pollution "rights" and taxi medallions.)

George followed his analysis with a plausible, practicable remedy: eliminate all taxes except for a tax on land values. The "single tax," as it later became known, would invigorate the economy by breaking up large idle holdings, making land available to those who would use it, and it would suck the air out of speculative bubbles, damping the boom and bust cycle. Taxing land is very progressive because land ownership is highly concentrated among the most wealthy, far more concentrated than income. Taxing land is fair, because the community rather than the individual landowner creates land values. Taxing land is economically efficient, because the owner cannot avoid a land tax ("shift" it) by choosing less-taxed options.

Both George's analysis and his remedy sprang directly from classical economic theory. Such giants as Adam Smith, David Ricardo, and John Stuart Mill, had already decried the evils of concentrated land ownership, which they called "land monopoly." George carried classical economics to its logical conclusion, and popularized that conclusion with stunning effect.

George emerged from a raw new colony, California, as a scrappy marginal journalist. Yet his ideas exploded through the sophisticated metropolitan world as into a vacuum. *Progress and Poverty* sold millions of copies worldwide, in dozens of translations, second only to the Bible. Returning from Ireland as reporter for *The Irish World* of New York, George was lionized by Irish New Yorkers for his stand on the Irish land question. With ethnic, union and socialist backing, he formed the United Labor Party in New York, and ran for mayor in 1886. Seven short years after leaving California, George nearly took over as Mayor of New York City, the financial and intellectual capital of the nation. He beat Theodore Roosevelt, but lost to the Tammany candidate, Abram S. Hewitt, by electoral fraud. In three more years, George had become a major influence in sophisticated Britain, as "adviser and field-general in land reform strategy" to the Radical wing of the Liberal Party. He was not even a British subject. In 1891, the Party adopted a land-tax plank, the "Newcastle Programme." Successive Liberal Governments of Campbell-Bannerman, Asquith, and Lloyd George carried forward modified "Georgist" policies. George toured the world as an immensely popular political activist, orator and folk hero. He died suddenly in 1897, while running a second time for Mayor of New York City. A hundred thousand mourners marched at his funeral.

In the US, "Georgism" melded into the populist movement, and later into the Progressive Movement. At the national level, the Progressive Movement dominated both major political parties for 17 years, 1902-19. At the local level, its influence continued through the early 1920s. Local property taxation was modified along Georgist lines: land assessments were raised relative to improvements and rates were increased substantially. California water districts financed by land taxes catapulted California to the top-producing farm state in the Union, using land that had been desert or range. California generated farm jobs and homes, while other states destroyed them by allowing well-connected speculators and "robber barons" to grab large tracts of land. A Georgist, Congressman Warren Worth Bailey of Pennsylvania, drafted the first Federal personal income tax law on Georgist lines: falling mainly on very high incomes from property.

In 1913 William S. U'Ren, "Father of the Initiative and Referendum," created this system of direct democracy expressly to push single-tax initiatives in Oregon. In 1910, as a by-product of U'Ren's single-tax campaigns, Oregon had adopted the first presidential primary law. This law was quickly imitated by many other states. The passage of these major electoral reforms during Woodrow Wilson's Governorship of New Jersey allowed him to win populist support and the Democratic nomination for President in 1912, and then defeat Taft. Wilson's mentor in New Jersey was an earnest Georgist, George L. Record. Record had gotten railroad lands up-taxed to the great benefit of public schools in New Jersey, and to the impoverishment of special-interest election funds. President Wilson included Georgists in his Cabinet (Newton D. Baker, Louis F. Post, Franklin K. Lane, and William B. Wilson), and collaborated with single-tax Congressmen like Henry George, Jr., and Warren Worth Bailey.

Joseph Fels, an idealistic American manufacturer, threw

himself and his fortune into the English land tax campaign, culminating in the Parliamentary revolution of 1909, which stripped the House of Lords of its power to veto tax bills. Subsequently, he threw millions into single-tax campaigns in the US. In 1916, a "pure single-tax" initiative, led by Luke North, won 31% of the votes in California. Even while "losing," campaigns like these kept the issue highly visible. Assessors consequently focused more attention on land. By 1917 in California, land value constituted 72% of the assessment roll for property taxation — a much higher fraction than today.

George's ideas were carried worldwide by such towering figures as David Lloyd George and George Bernard Shaw in England, Leo Tolstoy and Alexandr Kerensky in Russia, Sun Yat-Sen in China, Billy Hughes in Australia, Rolland O'Regan in New Zealand, Chaim Weizmann in Palestine, Francisco Madero in Mexico, and other leaders in Denmark, South Africa, and elsewhere around the world. In England, parts of Lloyd George's budget speech of 1909 could have been written by Henry George himself. Some of Winston Churchill's speeches were written by Georgist ghosts.

Twentieth century historians Raymond Moley and Eric Goldman emphasize George's impact. According to Moley, George "touched almost all of the corrective influences which were the result of the Progressive movement. The restriction of monopoly, more democratic political machinery, municipal reform, the elimination of privilege in railroads, the regulation of public utilities, and the improvement of labor laws and working conditions — all were... accelerated by George." According to Goldman, "George inspired most of the major reformers of the early 20th Century... no other book came anywhere near comparable influence... [it was] a volume which magically catalyzed the best yearnings of our grandfathers and fathers."

Where is the Georgist movement today?

World War I broke the momentum of the Progressive Movement in the US and the Liberal movement in England, allowing Georgist enemies to regroup. And enemies of course there were, because "Georgism" aims a dagger at the heart of unearned wealth and privilege. Enemies ultimately succeeded by a dual strategy. They tarred "Georgism" with the brush of Socialism or Communism, evoking images of the terrifying new regime in Russia. And they redefined economic theory, eliminating land as a significant category. In the US, the "robber barons" even financed the establishment of anti-Georgist economics departments at several major universities, including Columbia and Chicago.* Today an army of neo-classicists preach dourly that we must sacrifice equity on the altar of "efficiency." Thus they would stifle the demand for social justice that runs like a thread through the Bible, the Koran, and other great religious works.

Yet George's ideas are with us still. As historians often note, the Populist and Progressive movements faded out partly because they were co-opted by the leading parties. Ideas that we associate today with "liberal" Democrats — belief in the fairness of taxing "unearned" income, concern for "root causes" of poverty and unemployment, concern for social and racial justice — these ideas have strong Georgist roots. Likewise, ideas we associate today with free-market Republicans and Libertarians — the productive power of capitalism, the need for free trade, the need to liberate labor and capital from burdensome taxation and regulation — these ideas have equally strong Georgist roots.

There are also today's Georgist success stories, rarely recognized as such: the Asian "tigers": Taiwan, South Korea, Hong Kong and Singapore. Founded on the twin principles of access to land — implemented by land reform, land taxes and land leasing — and universal education and health care, the tigers' booming economies make them models for developing countries. Mainstream economists may have forgotten land taxes, but development economists still advocate them — circumspectly of course, lest they offend the third world rulers they hope to influence.

---

* a story detailed by the author in *The Corruption of Economics,* Shepheard-Walwyn, 1994.

Today, Georgists face both danger and opportunity:

Danger. The great Georgist reforms steadily erode, undefended by those who do not understand their significance. Property taxes, once the mainstay of local and state governments, increasingly give way to local and state sales and income taxes. Generations of propaganda have convinced even good liberals that property taxes fall squarely on the poor — to the mega-million dollar benefit of corporations like Standard Oil of California, the largest beneficiary of Proposition 13's 1979 property tax rollback and freeze. The federal income tax, which once targeted unearned income from land, now devolves steadily into a payroll tax.

Opportunity. Over the last twenty years, wealth and wages have grown ever more unequal, while the death of the Communist bogeyman reveals the ugliness of capitalism without fair laws or equal opportunity. Neo-classical economists, trundling through a "Mars-scape" of dusty statistics and forbidding formulas, can proffer only unpleasant trade-offs. In the debate over the 1997 income tax "reforms," Democrats complained that cuts in estate taxes and capital gains taxes for the rich were "unfair." Republicans argued, successfully, that such tax favors are essential to investment and growth.

Neoclassical economists give us only a hard choice: we may have equity, or efficiency, but not both. By contrast, George's program reconciles equity and efficiency. Think of it! George takes two polar philosophies, collectivism and individualism, and composes them into one solution. He cuts the Gordian knot. Like Keynes after him, George inspires us by saying, "Forget the bitter tradeoffs; we can have it all!"

— From a speech to the 1997 Council of Georgist Organizations conference commemorating the 100th anniversary of Henry George's death. Thanks to the Robert Schalkenbach Foundation.

Index

About the **Henry George Institute**

www.henrygeorge.org

The Institute is incorporated as a non-profit organization in New York State. Founded in 1971, it is a membership organization supported by dues and contributions. In the belief that the economic analysis of Henry George has important answers to today's urgent problems, the Institute is established to promote public awareness of these ideas. Its three-part distance learning course, *Principles of Political Economy,* is approved for college credit by the National College Credit Recommendation Service. The Henry George Institute has taught students in over 100 countries.

Made in the USA
Charleston, SC
29 November 2013